W9-BAH-471

REVIEW IS INSIDE LAST PAGE

THE TOTAL PENGUIN

THE PENGUIN IS AN
AMPHIBIOUS BIRD SO WELL
KNOWN TO MOST PEOPLE
THAT I SHALL ONLY
OBSERVE THAT THEY ARE
HERE IN PRODIGIOUS
NUMBERS AND WE COULD
KNOCK DOWN AS MANY AS
WE PLEASED WITH A STICK.
— Captain James Cook,
1775

THE TOTAL
PENGUIN

JAMES GORMAN

PHOTOGRAPHS BY FRANS LANTING

PRENTICE
HALL
EDITIONS

New York London Toronto Sydney Tokyo Singapore

PRENTICE HALL PRESS
15 Columbus Circle
New York, NY 10023

Copyright © 1990 by James
Gorman

Photographs copyright © 1990 by
Frans Lanting/Minden Pictures

PRENTICE HALL PRESS and
colophons are registered trade-
marks of Simon & Schuster, Inc.

Library of Congress Cataloging-
in-Publication Data

Gorman, James, 1949-
The total penguin/James
Gorman.
ISBN 0-13-925041-7 : $29.95
1. Penguins. I. Title.
QL696.S473G67 1990
598.441—dc20
89-48364
CIP

Designed by J.C. Suarès

Design Coordination by
Gates Studio

Manufactured in the United
States of America

10 9 8 7 6 5 4 3 2 1

First Edition

All photographs by Frans
Lanting except:

Department of Library Services,
American Museum of Natural
History: 18, 22, 74

Australian Tourist Commission:
28

© Leslie Jean-Bart: 180

Library of Congress: 1, 30–31,
52, 85

The Logical Society of
Philadelphia: 156

© New York Zoological Society
Photo: 5, 27, 96

© William Curtsinger, Photo
Researchers, Inc.: 165

Sea World, Inc.: 128

Zoological Society of San Diego:
167

© Anne Zuckerman, Eye on the
World: 2, 8–9

Map by George Colbert: 81

Illustrations by Peter Harrison,
SEABIRDS: An Identification
Guide, Croom Helm Publishers
Limited, 1983: 82-83

PAGE ONE: *Two Adélie penguins, with the icebound
ship* Belgica *in the background. On one of the first
Antarctic expeditions
(1897–99) the* Belgica *was
trapped in the ice below the
Antarctic Circle for almost
a year. It was the reports of
early explorers that popularized the Adélie penguin.*
PAGE TWO: *The author in
the company of penguins.
The place is Salisbury
Plain, South Georgia
Island, and the king pen-
guins in the background
number in the thousands.*

For my mother and father

The black-footed penguin
from southern Africa is
very common in zoos. It
walks with the slightly
unbalanced waddle of all
penguins.

FINALLY, THE QUESTION MAY BE ASKED, "WHAT GOOD ARE PENGUINS?" IT MAY BE CRASS TO ASK WHAT GOOD A WILD ANIMAL IS, BUT I DO THINK THE QUESTION MAY ALSO BE LEGITIMATE. THAT DEPENDS ON WHAT YOU MEAN BY GOOD. IF YOU MEAN "GOOD TO EAT," YOU ARE PERHAPS BEING STUPID. IF YOU MEAN "GOOD TO HUNT," YOU ARE SURELY BEING VICIOUS. IF YOU MEAN "GOOD AS IT IS GOOD IN ITSELF TO BE A LIVING CREATURE ENJOYING LIFE," YOU ARE NOT BEING CRASS, STUPID, OR VICIOUS. I AGREE WITH YOU AND I AM YOUR BROTHER AS WELL AS THE PENGUIN'S.

—George Gaylord
Simpson, *1976*

Contents

LEFT: *Gentoo penguins gather in a hillside colony on the Falkland Islands. They are on pastureland, which they share with sheep and browsing wild upland geese.*
OVERLEAF: Homo sapiens *and* Aptenodytes patagonica *together, an image that raises the question, all too often overlooked in the penguin literature, as to which creatures are, in fact, the silly ones.*

1 Dressed for Dinner

WITH SINGULAR
UNANIMITY, EXPLORERS
HAVE LIKENED THE
ADÉLIE PENGUIN TO
A SMART AND FUSSY
LITTLE MAN IN
EVENING CLOTHES.
— Robert Cushman
Murphy, *Oceanic
Birds of South
America*, 1936

About a month before I saw my first penguin in the wild I bought my first tuxedo. I was about to go to a party at which tuxedos were required, and I felt the time had come for me to stop renting them at the mall. Friends recommended that as long as I owned it I ought to bring it with me when I went in pursuit of penguins. Then I could add to what has become a small genre of travel photography—the snapshot of the tourist in his tuxedo, next to the penguins in theirs.

I demurred. Instead I filled my suitcase with a variety of different socks that I hoped would keep my feet warm when I stepped in puddles of glacial melt water and in the shallows of the chill ocean of Antarctica. Having now seen penguins, quite a lot of them, and thought, and read about them, I have given this dressed-up-penguin image quite a lot of my attention.

I've carefully inspected advertisements for Colombian coffee to see which penguin it is that is supposed to be all dressed up for some classy event (the king penguin). I've identified the species of *Spheniscus* penguin that is used to advertise a certain brand of innersoles meant to keep the feet dry. I've considered the development of formal dress for men and scrutinized the color schemes of all seventeen or eighteen species of penguins. I have asked myself, and a few other people, why penguins are universally loved. And I have stared at the birds themselves, in zoos, in the wild—all the while conscious of my mission. I don't know that I've thought about the *image* of penguins more than anybody else, but it's possible.

At first I was confused. I thought, as many people do, that penguins are black and white, and men in formal or semiformal dress wear black and white, and so they look alike. I thought it was as simple as that. Well, it's not. Not by a long shot.

RIGHT: *A group of Adélies, the penguins we all know as little men in dinner dress, ride an ice floe in the cold waters of the Weddell Sea. Adélies, among the most social of penguins, are almost always seen in groups.*

What we are talking about, when we talk about flightless marine birds as little men in dinner dress, is the interaction of biological evolution (in the penguins) and cultural evolution (in menswear). This image of the penguin represents nothing less (and nothing more either) than the serendipitous intersection, at a certain point in time, of natural selection and fashion.

Thus, the image of the penguin as a man in formal dress was not inevitable, although the notion that penguins look like nuns was (that's God's fault, and I'm not going to try to explain it). The image is purely accidental, a bit of colloquial metaphor tossed up as foam by the crosswinds of history and natural history. The image need not have emerged. There was much standing in its way. For instance, many of the penguins themselves might have stood in its way.

In the flesh, penguins are never quite as elegant, awkward, or comical as one expects them to be. They do not stand about holding drinks and colloquies. Rather, they stand around mating, pecking, and batting each other with their flippers like agitated toddlers. They clamber over rocks covered in their own guano, fall down in the stuff, regurgitate food for their young, and croak, bray, trumpet, and squawk as if they had no notion at all that we like to think of them as silly little people. They sometimes seem determined to act as if they were nothing but smelly, noisy, ill-tempered birds every bit as absorbed with their own petty struggles to eat, mate, and stay alive as we are with ours. Most of all they spend the greater part of their lives not standing at all, nor doing their trademark silly walk, but swimming, diving, and porpoising in the world's southern ocean waters as the marine creatures they really are. In the water, I might point out, they look neither like men nor birds.

Furthermore—and I say this with regret for those readers who don't know it, because I know it will hit hard at first—not all penguins are pure black and white. Ornithologists disagree on exactly how many species of penguins there are—one bird man's, or woman's, species is another's subspecies—but most say seventeen or eighteen. These penguins are scattered about the shores of the islands and continents of the Southern Hemisphere, and though a penguin of any species is obviously

RIGHT: *Rock hoppers in the Falkland Islands. Rock hoppers are among the most numerous of penguins. On one island in the Falkland group they gather in the millions.*

a penguin, there are significant variations. Consider the crested penguins, which deserve far more popular acclaim than they now receive. They do have the traditional dark back and white belly. But above their eyes they also have long, fringed, yellow feathers, creating the impression of wildly garish eyebrows. Officially, these tufted decorations are called *aigrettes*. That's all well and good if you're an ornithologist, but few of us are. I think a more expressive term for these feathers would be lunatic fringe, as in "the rock hopper, smallest of the crested penguins, has a particularly noticeable lunatic fringe."

The rock hoppers, *Eudyptes crestatus*, are my favorite penguins. They're only about a foot high, but they're aggressive birds with a personality reminiscent of a small male terrier, or of Kipling's indefatigable mongoose, Rikki-tikki-tavi. Explorers

ABOVE: *The chinstrap is the only penguin to have something approximating a black tie to go with its white shirt and black coat. Most penguins are more appropriately said to be attired in white tie and tails.*

tell of merciless and fearless attacks on human interlopers in a rock-hopper colony, of ship's dogs driven mad after wandering among the birds on their nests, and of these penguins leaping, enraged, into the air to attach themselves to an invader's sleeve and hanging on with clamped bill while swung about in the air. (I myself have seen rock hoppers, but, I regret to say, did not get a chance to swing them about in this way.) The rock hoppers also have, in addition to their lunatic fringe, spiked black feathers on the top of their heads and glowing red eyes, like Rikki-tikki-tavi's. (In case you hadn't guessed, of all characters in literature, Rikki-tikki-tavi is my favorite.) Not to lose sight of the thrust of the argument here, let me point out that these birds do not appear to be dressed for a dinner dance.

The king penguins are at the other end of penguin style. Like all penguins they

ABOVE: *The rock hopper penguin, with its red eyes, spiked black feathers on the top of its head, and yellow tufted eyebrows, gives a different image than the little man in formal dress. Only a foot high, these birds can be as aggressive as their looks would suggest.*

have a comic side, but they also have grandeur and stature. Aristotle, in his *Poetics*, prescribes for the comic playwright the use of low and vulgar creatures. In general, penguins fit this bill admirably. But the kings are an exception. They are sometimes vulgar, but never low. In fact, they are quite tall—around three feet to the tops of their velvet-black heads. They have silver backs and richly colored yellow neck patches. Robert Cushman Murphy, who first saw these animals on South Georgia Island in 1912, when he was a twenty-six-year-old naturalist, wrote that he had seen no other birds as magnificent. Roger Tory Peterson, another man who has seen his share of birds, including all varieties of penguin in the wild, has written that of all the birds the king penguin is his favorite. (It seems that famous ornithologists, like famous blues singers, must have three names—John James Audubon is another.) I stood next to these penguins in the thousands on the same island that

BELOW: *An old shelter on Bounty Island off New Zealand, once used by wrecked sailors, is now frequented by penguins.*

Murphy and Peterson visited, and it seems to me that Murphy captured best the experience of looking at them for the first time. He wrote, "The movements of their white breasts and golden gorgets stir me as the daffodils stirred Wordsworth." Of the rock hoppers he later wrote, "Picture a penguin, smaller than any of the preceding kinds [he had already discussed several others], with a yellow pompon over each eye, and a gait that caused the early visitors to the Falkland Islands to dub it the 'Jumping Jack.'... Instead of walking, it progresses in 'a series of bounds executed with ... an elasticity of motion such as is exhibited by kangaroos.' " I had forgotten to mention that they do indeed hop rocks.

Neither of these birds would have given rise to the image of a man in formal dress. Nor would the yellow-eyed penguins (also known among the cognoscenti as YEPs or Chookies), solitary nesters in the forests of New Zealand, or many of the other species have done so. However, the image has thrived for years, dominating the popular consciousness of penguins and thoroughly resistant to the heterogeneity of penguin reality. So, which bird is it? Which one is dressed for dinner? As Murphy said in the quote that fronts this chapter, it is the Adélie. All in black and white, with a most comical shape and waddle, given to curiosity and not overly aggressive, an Adélie does indeed look like a man wearing, not a tuxedo, but white tie and tails. To be even more precise, an Adélie looks like a man in white tie and tails with incredibly short legs. It is as if his black shoes come right out of his boiled shirt.

Protective Coloration

The primary ingredient in the image is, of course, the coloration. I do not subscribe to the notion that nothing in nature is accidental. On the other hand, many natural phenomena, like the coloration of penguins, clearly evolved because of natural selection. There is a reason why Adélies are black and white just as there is a reason why men wear formal dress. In fact, it's the same reason—protective coloration. One creature does it to be less visible to predators in the water, the other

OVERLEAF: *Rock hoppers, slick from the sea, begin to walk, or rather, hop, home. Some rock hopper colonies number in the millions.*

to avoid wearing the wrong clothes to a dinner party, a fate some might consider on a par with being eaten by a leopard seal.

But coloration in and of itself is not enough. To be sure, the Adélie wears the colors of a headwaiter (and all penguins have, at the least, dark backs and white fronts), but so do many other seabirds. The auks, auklets, and murres, sometimes called the penguins of the Northern Hemisphere, are by and large black and white. The blue-eyed shag, which nests on the same islands as Adélie penguins, has a dark back and a white belly. All of these birds face predators who may be coming from either above or below them in the sea. Looking up from deeper water into the light, a seal or shark is likely to have a hard time picking a white belly out of the brightness. Looking down from the surface into deeper water, the same predator will find it difficult to spot a black back.

And yet, no one that I know of has waxed friendly and metaphorical about the blue-eyed shag. One might say that this is because blue-eyed shags are cor-

ABOVE: *Roald Amundsen, who led the first expedition to reach the South Pole, approaching Adélie penguins. This was during an earlier expedition to Antarctica, when he was a mate on board the* Belgica *1897–99. The expedition was trapped in the ice for almost a year and fought scurvy with fresh seal and penguin meat.*

RIGHT: *The Galápagos penguin, one of the rarest and smallest, lives on the islands near the equator that gave it its name. It is the penguin that lives farthest north, far from Antarctic lands and seas.*

morants, and nobody likes a cormorant, much. But that begs the question. Why *don't* people like cormorants? Well, I can think of one reason—poor posture. Both cormorants and shags, like most other birds, have a strange tilt to their upper bodies, and proceed, when they have to get about on land, with torsos tilted and necks crooked, rather than honest and upright, as God intended for bipedal creatures to walk.

Penguins, however, stand and walk with backs as straight as those of butlers. The anthropocentric explanation for this walk is that they have self-respect. The real reason, as with almost everything in penguin life, has to do with the water. In order for penguins to swim well and efficiently under water, they needed to develop a streamlined shape. And they have. The front end is pointed; the body gradually swells; and the feet are tucked away behind the body, not sticking down and dragging. (Penguins propel themselves with their wings or flippers, not their feet.) Evolution of a streamlined diver and swimmer produced, coincidentally, something that looked a little bit like a clumsy man. But this awkwardness didn't matter. Penguins have never had to deal with significant predation, or criticism, on land. As long as they can get up on land to breed and get in and out of the water to feed, how they get around, much less how they look doing it, is supremely unimportant.

That is the penguin's side of the tuxedo story. In sum, the pressures of natural selection produced a slightly bottom-heavy, upright, black-and-white bird that lived far south, on and around the Antarctic Continent for thousands and thousands of years as it waited for people who also dressed properly to come and make it into a clown.

In considering the people, we must turn for a moment of seriousness (a brief one, I promise) to Keith Thomas's *Man and the Natural World: A History of the Modern Sensibility*. Thomas writes: "The work of many anthropologists suggests that it is an enduring tendency of human thought to project upon the natural world (and

---

PRECEDING OVERLEAF: *Kings, perhaps the most beautiful of penguins, incubate their eggs on their feet under a flap of skin. The ornithologist Robert Cushman Murphy wrote of these birds, "The movement of their white breasts and golden gorgets stir me as the daffodils stirred Wordsworth."*

particularly the animal kingdom) categories and values derived from human society and then to serve them back as a critique or reinforcement of the human order."

Dr. Thomas is a serious person, and he was talking about fashions in politics rather than dress. Bees at one time were seen to represent the smooth functioning

ABOVE: *Two Adélies calling to each other. Some writers have waxed romantic about penguin courtships, one describing the birds "doing a great deal of love-making, becoming vastly sentimental in the process."*

of monarchy and to provide a justification that this form of government was natural. At another time the societies of beavers, storks, rooks, and cranes were thought to be republican in nature. Just as people could not have imagined king bees (only later did they discover they were really queens) until they had created kings among themselves, so people could not have imagined penguins to appear to be wearing evening dress until the germane "categories and values"—white tie and tails—had been invented. In fact, I suspect that there also had to be some ambivalence about evening dress already in existence, some sense that perhaps it was a trifle silly or stiff, before penguins could be seen to be wearing it. I doubt if a form of dress uniformly judged to be elegant, associated with a class of people uniformly respected, admired, and confident about themselves, would have come to be associated with

---

ABOVE: *Little blue, or fairy, penguins on an Australian beach, caught by the light of a flash. They are the smallest penguins, the only ones to nest on the continent of Australia, and the only nocturnal penguins.*

creatures that waddle and squawk and have no more sense of restraint about their bodily functions than did the court at Versailles.

I have not been able to pin down the exact moment at which the image of the formally attired penguin first appeared. There are no concordances of metaphorical descriptions of animals that I know of. And though I have read a fair amount of penguin literature, I have by no means read it all. It is not as if this (whatever this is) is an active field of scholarship. In general, there are books on clothing and books on animals, and there is precious little overlap.

Nonetheless, I have been able to puzzle out a few things. First of all, the very early European observers of penguins, such as Antonio Pigafetta, who traveled with Magellan on the world's first circumnavigation, tended to compare penguins not to men in tails but to other animals, usually geese. I believe this is partly because the early maritime explorers were frequently starving, and it was the culinary, far more than the comical, aspects of penguins with which they were preoccupied. More important (the later explorers were often starving too) was that in Magellan's day one didn't wear white tie and tails. I'm not sure exactly what one did wear, but I believe it was more colorful and involved very tight pants for the men.

Penguins *were* compared to human beings and human fashions in the late 1700s. The penguin in question was the macaroni, one of the crested penguins, whose fringe I described earlier. According to George Gaylord Simpson, one of the great paleontologists of this century, who also had a passion for penguins, sailors named the macaroni after a group of notorious English fops who sported a particularly fancy hairdo. This group is described in *Muffs and Morals* (one of those clothing books that doesn't talk about animals):

> The London Macaroni Club was at its height in 1772, a playboy club for
> young gentlemen who had made the Grand Tour and returned to England
> with a passion for Italy and everything Italian. They favoured a style of

OVERLEAF: *A lone emperor penguin gives the impression of dignity (and a head a size or so too small for its enormous body) for which the birds are known. In the background is the* Belgica *from its 1897–99 Antarctic expedition.*

dress with pouter-pigeon bosom, cravat swathed over the chin, skimpy white silk breeches worn extremely tight and giving the effect of bow legs. Besides these unmistakeable signs, a Macaroni distinguished himself from others by his very high wig, on the top of which was perched a tiny hat, which he raised in salute by means of a tall cane.

As Simpson points out, the American colonial song "Yankee Doodle" makes reference to the attire of these London dandies in the line, "stuck a feather in his cap and called it macaroni."

It was not until Victorian times that the formal dress now accepted in the Western world came into vogue. It was in the 1850s that the cutaway coat became restricted to use as evening wear. Toward the end of the century, evening dress was divided into the formal white tie and tails, and the less formal dinner jacket, both worn with stiff white shirts. Daytime formal dress for men was, and I suppose still is, a morning coat with striped trousers, and a stiff white shirt. This is the sort of outfit worn by people who attend the Ascot races, or get their wedding pictures in the society pages of the *New York Times*, or both.

The attentive reader will notice that the work *tuxedo* has not appeared in this account of sartorial development. The word *tuxedo* is an Americanism meaning "dinner jacket," and it comes from a club in an eponymous New York suburb, which in turn was named after a tribe of Indians. Or, to quote *Famous First Facts* (the sort of book that interdisciplinary scholars like myself are often forced to rely on), "The tuxedo coat is said to have been introduced from England by Griswold Lorillard, who wore a tailless dress coat and waistcoat of scarlet satin at the Tuxedo Club, Tuxedo Park, N.Y., on October 10, 1886."

Thus, the two primary ingredients in the evolution of the penguin's current image were the penguins themselves and human beings who knew how to dress.

PRECEDING OVERLEAF: *A band of gentoo penguins, flippers out, returns from the sea. The undersides of the flippers are flushed pink from increased blood flow, which helps the birds shed heat.*
LEFT: *A sleeping rock hopper, eyes closed, has its head tucked under a flipper. Like other birds when they are resting, penguins will duck their heads under their wings.*

The first had existed for tens of millions of years before the humans reached a suitable level of sartorial evolution. The mixing of these ingredients finally occurred, so it seems, with the Antarctic expeditions of men like Robert Falcon Scott, Roald Amundsen, and Ernest Shackleton. These were all men who knew of, indeed, often *wore* evening dress, and who saw plenty of Adélie penguins. The result, as Robert Cushman Murphy wrote, is that, "Popularly speaking, [the Adélie] is the type and epitome of the penguin family, a prestige developed entirely during the period of active south-polar exploration that began after the opening of the present century."

The earliest written references to dressed-up penguins that I've run across suggest that the idea was already so well known as to be obvious. Edward Wilson, who accompanied Robert Falcon Scott on both his expeditions to the Antarctic, and died with him on the second, offers many superb descriptions of penguins in the diaries he kept for both trips, accounts that are both poetic and precise. In his entry for December 11, 1910, early in the second trip, he writes, "Now and again one hears a penguin cry out in the stillness near at hand or far away, and then, perhaps he appears in his dress tail coat and white waistcoat suddenly upon an ice floe from the water."

Later, the image became so common that everyone (I know I am no exception) had to analyze and improve it. Cherry Kearton, in the 1931 book *The Island of Penguins*, says, "It is usual, when writing of penguins, to say … that they are like men in dress coats; and to compare their front view to a white shirt and white waistcoat, white trousers and black shoes." Kearton's book is full of interesting anecdotes, but in places is so relentless in its anthropomorphism (in this regard no creature poses a greater temptation than the penguin) as to make one wish for the dry, indigestible prose of a scientific paper. Describing a reunion, after a hard day, of "Mr. and Mrs. Penguin," Kearton writes:

> He tries to break into a run, nearly falls over in his eagerness, stops for a moment to think how beautiful she is, and then, coming nearer, he leans down to put his head affectionately against hers. Then he goes into the hole

RIGHT: *King penguins, apparently engaged in philosophy, share the land with an elephant seal. The glaciated mountains of South Georgia rise in the background.*

beside her, caresses her, and embraces her with his flippers. How good it is to be home again, feeling so comfortably well fed, and to have such an adorable wife awaiting him!

Kearton goes on to say that Mr. and Mrs. Penguin do a "great deal of love-making, becoming vastly sentimental in the process," a condition that was apparently infectious.

Cuteness: Penguins, Bunnies, and Babies

Mr. and Mrs. Penguin bring up an aspect of the popular image of penguins that is connected to, but not quite the same as, the wearing of evening clothes: cuteness. Kearton's penguins are insufferably cute. Real penguins, although not reaching quite this level of appeal, are also cute, and silly—which is a corollary quality. It was probably necessary for penguins to be cute for us to see them as fussy little men in tuxedos, but it is not exactly the same thing. Cuteness is not a function of coloration. Killer whales are black and white, and they are not cute. Nor is it a result of posture. Kodiak bears often walk upright, and they are not cute. You can even put the two together—a black-and-white Kodiak bear standing upright, all twelve feet of him—and you still don't get cute.

I'm not fooling around here. I'm using the word *cute* in its technical, scientific sense. We may think we know what cute is. Bunnies and babies are cute, rats and lizards are not. But this is only a working, operational definition. For the theory of cute we must turn to Konrad Lorenz, the late Nobel prize–winning animal behaviorist. He suggested that certain features of human babies release our maternal and paternal impulses, our desire to care for our young. When we see the same features in other creatures, he said, we feel the same way we do about our human infants: that they are *cute*. Lorenz included among the features that trigger the "oohs" and "ahhs" that are always heard in the presence of puppies, "a relatively large head, predominance of the brain capsule, large and low-lying eyes, bulging cheek region, short and thick extremities, a springy elastic consistency, and clumsy movements."

I am not the first to transpose this theory into the realm of popular culture. Indeed, I was alerted to Lorenz's formula in an essay on Mickey Mouse by paleontologist

Stephen Jay Gould. Gould pointed out that Mickey's character became cuter and cuter over the years. And as it did, Mickey's creators changed his physical appearance. The mouse evolved from a true pointy-nosed, beady-eyed rodent into something considerably more bunnylike. His illustrators gave him, over time, a bigger head, bigger eyes, fatter cheeks, and a shorter nose.

When one tries to fit penguins to the Lorenz formula, the results are at first inconclusive. Their heads and eyes vary in size—some are large, some are only big enough to avoid embarrassment. Judging from the comments on the rock hoppers that I quoted earlier, their consistency is elastic enough, although I have no personal opinion on this matter. Certainly, with their flippers at their sides, and their very short legs, penguins give the impression of a large torso and "short and thick extremities." But it is when we come to clumsy movements that they truly shine. Penguins are to clumsiness what Paganini was to dexterity. They are the *ne plus ultra* of waddle. Not even John Cleese's Minister Of Silly Walks surpasses them. They stumble, they fall, they slide, they use their bills to push themselves up. We compare them unfavorably to ourselves, of course, since we both walk upright. But there is more than anthropomorphism at work here. Penguins may be tough and agile, and they may climb extraordinarily slippery, steep rock faces with remarkable agility. But the sight of birds that have fallen so many times that they are covered with their own guano is so common in a penguin colony that the most objective observer would have to conclude that these are birds that walk not wisely, and not too well, either.

To coloration and bipedal clumsiness we might also add behavior. Penguins exhibit great curiosity and lack of fear. (Again, the Adélie is the archetype. Some other varieties of penguins are terrified of people—and with good reason, but that is a subject for later on.) Adélies will waddle toward human beings with what seems to be a kind of pushy innocence. In this they are very similar to other people's children. Also, since penguins are nearsighted and have little or no binocular vision, they are given

OVERLEAF: *Relations between seals and penguins are not always peaceable. In fact, leopard seals are major predators of Adélie penguins. Here a southern sea lion on a Falkland Islands' beach has snatched a gentoo.*

to a kind of clumsiness apart from the way they walk. They tilt their heads this way and that, looking literally cockeyed, to give this or that eye a good view.

The end result is that they appear to us to be ridiculous. Their awkwardness is juxtaposed against a picture of utmost formality, a sure comic combination. Robert Falcon Scott's description of a group of Adélies captures perfectly the flavor of this view of penguins:

> Tonight we are camped near some rocks half way towards the ice-edge; there are several seals close by, and small bands of Adélie penguins are constantly passing us. It is curious there should be so many, as we know of no rookery near, and it is still more curious why they should be making south, as there is no open water beyond the few cracks near the land. It gives us the idea that they don't quite know what they are doing, especially since we watched the movements of one small band; they were travelling towards the south with every appearance of being in a desperate hurry—flippers outspread, heads bent forward, and little feet going for all they were worth. Their business-like air was intensely ludicrous; one could imagine them saying in the fussiest manner, "Can't stop to talk now, much too busy."

The ironies of history are cruel, and instructive. It is only to us that the penguins seem silly. They actually get along quite well in what are, to say the least, difficult circumstances. Scott, on the other hand, died in what a penguin might well describe as an intensely ludicrous activity (as if penguins cared): trying to walk to the South Pole for no other reason than to be there first. Furthermore, new work on Scott suggests that he lost his own life and those of four of his men because of bad planning and arrogance. In the light of this history, one cannot help but think of his

---

PRECEDING OVERLEAF: *Giant petrels, a bird sometimes referred to as "Uncle Nasty," gather around a southern sea lion, waiting for offal, as the animal tears a penguin apart, ripping off the tough, feathered skin.*
LEFT: *Seals do not always get their prey. This king penguin has narrowly escaped from a seal and has returned to land, badly wounded and bloodied, but, for the moment, still alive.*

small band traveling south in a desperate hurry. There seems no doubt now about which group it was that didn't quite know what they were doing.

Cigarettes, Coffee, and Orchestras

Thus, the penguin we know and love and see endlessly on greeting cards, in cartoons, and in children's books. A serendipitous confluence of culture, exploration, protective coloration, and upright posture gave us the silly little man in evening clothes, the universal penguin, the image against which all other penguins are measured. Once it appeared in our consciousness, this irresistibly cute, shuffling headwaiter, this epitome of avian comedy, quite naturally made its way into popular culture.

Penguins are not as common as dogs or cats or rabbits in cartoons and comic strips, movies and advertisements. But they are there. They may not be as ubiquitous in knickknack form as ducks or frogs, but they are there. On a tourist cruise to penguin-rich islands, I met a number of penguin aficionados. One of them had begun in childhood with a pair of penguin pajamas and continued through gifts and impulsive acquisitions until penguins had become her *thing*. At the time of the trip, during which she was seeing her first wild penguins, she estimated her penguin objects at somewhere near a thousand in number. Perhaps the best penguin object or set of objects that I have heard of (belonging to another collector, reputedly the owner of penguin things in the several thousands) is a set of bowling pins made in the form of penguins. Set 'em up. Knock 'em down. Captain Cook would have loved them.

As to the penguins that belong to us all, there are no truly famous movie penguins, no bird to rival Rin Tin Tin or Trigger, or even Bonzo (the chimpanzee who starred with Ronald Reagan in *Bedtime for Bonzo*). But there was Percy the Penguin, who was in *My Favorite Blonde* with Bob Hope and Madeleine Carroll (1942). Two king penguins almost killed by a fishing boat have starred in Diet Coke commercials. Naturally, the penguins took the roles, in one of the commercials, of waiters in tuxedos. The trays were strapped to the birds, who kept pecking at them. The penguins broke eleven different kinds of trays before one strong enough was found. Penguins are tough birds.

And there are the penguins of the imagination, which have appeared in comic strips and advertisements. For years, Willie the Penguin was, appropriately, the symbol of Kool cigarettes. Willie, a remnant of the advertising style of the forties and fifties, suffers grievously from the fate that afflicts all animals that appear to be of illustrative use, from dinosaurs to bears to mice—he loses his shape.

His true shape, that is. Naturally, Willie is drawn for effect, without regard to the actual structure of penguins. Some of his modifications I find understandable, even appealing. His cue-ball head is not without charm. The stylized cone-shaped beak, with the cigarette hanging from it, Bogart style, does indeed make me want to smoke. And the frogman flippers he is given for feet are too witty to quibble over. But his wings (also called flippers) are an indignity. Willie is given boneless, snakelike appendages for wings, presumably to enable him to hold cartons of Kools and Santa masks, straight razors and strops, bows and arrows, soap and back scrubbers, all of which he clutches in one old advertisement or another. Such wings would not be of much use to him in life. Poor Willie.

In reality, penguin wings or flippers are stiff and hard and are covered with very small, densely packed feathers. They feel a bit like paddles, and penguins propel themselves underwater by moving these wings in a flying motion. When penguins are not using their flippers (wings) to swim, they often use them to hit each other. Edward Wilson described penguins using their flippers to good effect on both invading Englishmen and colony mates. Of king penguins he wrote in his diary, "The row was deafening. One had to shout orders to the men, and whenever a bird thought one was going to disturb it, it whacked out with both flippers and caught one tremendous blows, in fact the flippers are its best weapons by a long way." And later in the same diary entry, speaking of a group of crested penguins, he notes, "Extraordinarily quarrelsome and jealous they are too, for they nest so close together that when a bird wants to walk about, it gets pecked on each side by the birds squatting on their nests. And as it walks, it keeps its flippers going hard, and

---

OVERLEAF: *A group of rock hopper penguins preening and resting on a guano-stained rock ledge in the Falkland Islands. The birds acquired their name from their habit of hopping from rock to rock as they move up, or down, the rough cliffs they favor for their colonies.*

hits everybody on its way on both sides. Often the flippers of one bird come smack against those of another, with a loud clap."

Only a short bit later, again in the same entry, Wilson makes a comment that aptly captures the contradictions in human attitudes toward penguins, and indeed toward all other forms of life on the planet: "I spent my whole time among these penguins—they were so immensely fascinating. Besides, I had to kill all that were wanted, no one else killed any at all. It was rather a butchery, because we wanted some for food as well as for collecting. But I know they all pegged out as painlessly as it was possible to manage, and we have excellent skins too to send home."

I suppose one would expect that the uses to which metaphorized, mythologized, and structurally perverted penguins are put by popular culture are all purely visual. Neither television nor magazines nor billboards deal in sounds and smells. Just as well. A full sensual impression of penguins, complete with noise and odors, would be of no commercial use. A magazine advertisement for Colombian coffee, for example, which features king penguins, depends on the certainty that very few readers will have set foot in a king penguin colony. The caption reads, "You can always tell a Colombian coffee party by the way the crowd is dressed." Presumably, the elegant birds are meant to make one think of an elegantly set table, perhaps even of the rich aroma of freshly brewed coffee. And yet, consider Wilson's description of the colony of kings he visited: "All was stinking mud and in this wet filth the King Penguins were living and breeding." Personally, I think the kings are among the cleaner-living penguins.

A maker of innersoles has used penguins to advertise some of its products that keep one's feet dry and warm, which seems particularly curious to me. Penguins have wet feet far more often than dry, and they actually don't keep them warm. Rather, they save energy by living with cold feet, keeping them just above frostbite temperature but not wasting any unnecessary heating energy on unfeathered and thus uninsulated toes. I doubt that if we could ask them, the birds would say that they *feel* that their feet are cold, but this is not the sort of problem that is easy to address, scientifically, or that is likely to draw funding from the National Science Foundation.

In captivity, wet feet are another matter altogether, a big problem for penguins and other seabirds, often leading to bacterial infections grouped under the general category of *bumblefoot*. When I learned about this syndrome, I was very disappointed that such an evocative term had been wasted on a phenomenon as dreary as a bacterial infection. The word would have been perfect to describe the way penguins, all penguins, waddle along—bumblefooted.

A penguin is the logo of a well-known book publisher—Penguin Books. Penguins appear on greeting cards. They are drawn wearing Arctic Hats to keep heads warm. They are the tuxedoed mascots of the New York Philharmonic, appearing on the T-shirts, tote bags, and other accessories that all nonprofit institutions now seem to sell so that supporters can display the emblems of their good works and affections.

And penguins, perhaps because of their perceived affinity for ice and snow, and their habit of sliding about in groups and pecking and hitting each other, have been chosen as mascots by several hockey teams. (I don't know of any cases of penguins that learned to ice skate successfully. But at least two penguins learned to roller skate: the aforementioned Percy of movie fame, and a penguin who carried a mail bag at Sea World in San Diego.) Two of these hockey teams had a perfectly good reason for choosing penguins—the tuxedo/tails connection. The hockey teams, or perhaps clubs, from both the Juilliard School and the New England Conservatory call themselves the Penguins. Each year they meet in the Maestro Match. In the 1987 game, which Juilliard won, 15–2, the other Penguins' pep band played bits of Strauss and Mahler.

Penguins are also the mascot of a much more serious hockey team, in which lies another story about penguin personality and morphology. When the former Pittsburgh Hornets were renamed during the 1966–67 season, the coach threatened to resign over the new name. And in the first season as the Penguins, the players' jerseys showed no creature at all. The next season the bird appeared. In 1989 the team was in the playoffs against Philadelphia, which led to truly wonderful headlines for anyone fond of flightless waddlers, such as "Penguins Beat Flyers." Most interesting to me, however, is how the jersey designer for the team modified the penguin in order to make it look tougher. Naturally the bird wears skates and has arms instead of flippers that end in gloves holding a hockey stick. It also has something of a mean, aggressive look.

Now, although penguins may be mean and aggressive, most of them don't look it. The team could have chosen to be called the rock hoppers, of course, but apparently the National Hockey League is not that ornithologically sophisticated. I don't say this as a put-down—I don't think football or basketball is any better. (Baseball, maybe. They've got Cardinals, Blue Jays, and Orioles, after all. There are no seabirds, but there are Mariners.) What Pittsburgh picked was a generic penguin, a caricature of the ubiquitous Adélie. The bird was given pure black-and-white coloration, a moderately evil eye, and a rapacious-looking bill. I was puzzled at first about this nasty beak, but then I checked my bird books and I recognized it. In their wisdom, the Pittsburgh Penguins have attached to their emblem the beak of another black-and-white bird of the cold southern seas, though one less cute and far less well loved. The Pittsburgh Penguin has the beak of a blue-eyed shag.

ABOVE: *Emperor penguins were frequently encountered by early explorers and sometimes taken on board ship. Some were destined for the pot; others ended up as scientific specimens.*

I mentioned at the outset that I had not brought my tuxedo with me when I went south to visit penguins in the wild. Many other travelers have. Tourism to penguin-rich regions of the globe is burgeoning, and with it, the prevalence of the photograph of the traveler in tux or tails among the penguins. Usually, such pictures are only appealing if you happen to be a blood relative of the traveler. But not always.

This genre reached its apotheosis not long ago in a large panoramic picture of the king penguins of South Georgia Island that originally appeared in *Life* magazine. Standing among the thousands of birds was Zubin Mehta, who was at that time on sabbatical as music director of the New York Philharmonic. He was wielding his conducting baton, and he was quoted as saying, "I finally found enough musicians to play Mahler's Eighth Symphony."

There they are—the penguins of our imagination at their best—thousands of them dressed to the bills. They are appealing, puzzling, and irresistible enough that one is happy to set aside, for the moment, whatever it is that they really are. But only for the moment. A pursuit of penguins, which is what this book is, after all, can begin with the way most of us think of penguins: as fussy little men in evening clothes. But it must soon move on to reality—where birds are birds and one hopes Zubin Mehta was wearing rubber boots. The reality is not unrelated to our favorite image, but it is different. On South Georgia, for instance, where Murphy and Peterson visited the kings, and where Zubin Mehta had his picture taken, the birds that gather in the tens of thousands do indeed make a kind of music. But it's not Mahler.

OVERLEAF: *On the Falkland Islands, a young gentoo chick is sprawled, sleeping, on a sunny day. The gentoos range from the extreme climate of the Antarctic Islands to cold, temperate locales like the Falklands.*

2 The Real Penguins

> PENGUINS ARE
> STOCKY FLIGHTLESS
> HIGHLY AQUATIC
> BIRDS WITH DARK
> UPPERPARTS AND
> WHITE UNDERPARTS.
> — George E.
> Watson, *Birds of the*
> *Antarctic and Sub-*
> *Antarctic*, 1975

The kings trumpet. Or at least that's how their call is usually described. It is music of a sort, to the generous ear. Certainly it is something more than noise, a drawn-out, brassy horn sound with a slight, puzzling undertone or distortion, a built-in dissonance that makes the call sound like that of a Tibetan throat singer producing two notes from one larynx, or a television alien, with a voice electronically distorted to seem otherworldly. Other penguins make music too, or sounds, at any rate. The several sorts of jackass penguin bray. The rock hoppers and chinstraps and Adélies all have species-specific squawks, identifiable by another penguin or an ornithologist. Edward Wilson described the Adélie as crying "Ark! Ark!," a noise that appeared later in the children's book *Mr. Popper's Penguins.* As to rock hoppers, Robert Cushman Murphy paraphrases a member of an early scientific expedition when he says this penguin's call can be compared "only to something between the last notes of an ass's bray and the bleat of a deep-voiced sheep."

The calls of penguins are by no means insignificant. To the birds themselves, they serve to identify parents and children, to announce amorous or aggressive intentions, or simply to produce news of oneself. But they are also important for other, less subtle reasons. On the casual visitor, the calls of penguins have a powerful effect in readjusting one's sense of just what these birds are like. Noise is one of the two overwhelming realities of a penguin colony. When thousands of birds proclaim news of themselves at the same time, the effect is overwhelming.

Then, to get the full effect, add the impact on another sense, the other, overwhelming reality of colonial penguin life—the odor of excrement. On land, where they come to

---

RIGHT: *A rock hopper lets loose with its trademark cry, which one observer described as "something between the last notes of an ass's bray and the bleat of a deep-voiced sheep."*
OVERLEAF: *Nelson Island off the Antarctic Peninsula—crawling, or, more accurately, waddling, with penguins—is an example of the spare, roughhewn lands on which Antarctic penguins mate, nest, and raise their young.*

mate, colonial penguins gather in huge aggregations, sometimes numbering in the millions. (In 1965 the naturalist Ian Strange estimated that on Beauchene Island in the Falklands there were 2.5 million nests of rock hoppers. The density was more than two nests per square meter.) Penguins do not dig latrines. They do not have portable toilets of the sort popular at outdoor concerts. They do not go down to the sea or walk off into the woods to relieve themselves. (Usually there are no woods.) They simply stand in their own accumulating guano. The guano stains of penguin colonies can be seen from the sea long before the birds themselves are visible. Satellites in space can identify large penguin colonies by the pink or white guano patches on dark rock. Anyone with a nose, approaching an island on a ship, can smell a penguin colony from well offshore.

The reports of the *HMS Challenger* expedition landing on one of the islands of Tristan da Cunha in the South Atlantic give a vivid picture of a rock-hopper colony in a terrain covered with high tussock grass:

> A plunge is made into one of the lanes in the tall grass, which at once shuts out the surroundings from view. You tread on a slimy black damp soil composed of the birds' dung. The stench is overpowering, the yelling of the birds most annoying and discordant.... The nests are placed so thickly that you cannot help treading on eggs and young birds at almost every step. A parent bird sits on each nest with its sharp beak erect and open, ready to bite, yelling savagely, "caa, caa, urr, urr," its red eyes gleaming and its plumes at half-cock, quivering with rage. No sooner are your legs within reach than they are furiously bitten, often by two or three birds at once.... At first you try to avoid the nests, but soon find that impossible; then maddened almost, by the pain, stench, and noise, you have recourse to brute force. Thump, thump goes your stick, and at each blow down goes a bird.... and the path behind you is strewed with the dead and dying and bleeding.

Had Dante known of penguins, Hell might have had another level.

RIGHT: *Macaroni penguins, alpinists in their choice of nesting sites, cover the rocks of a steep and jagged cliff in shocking profusion.*

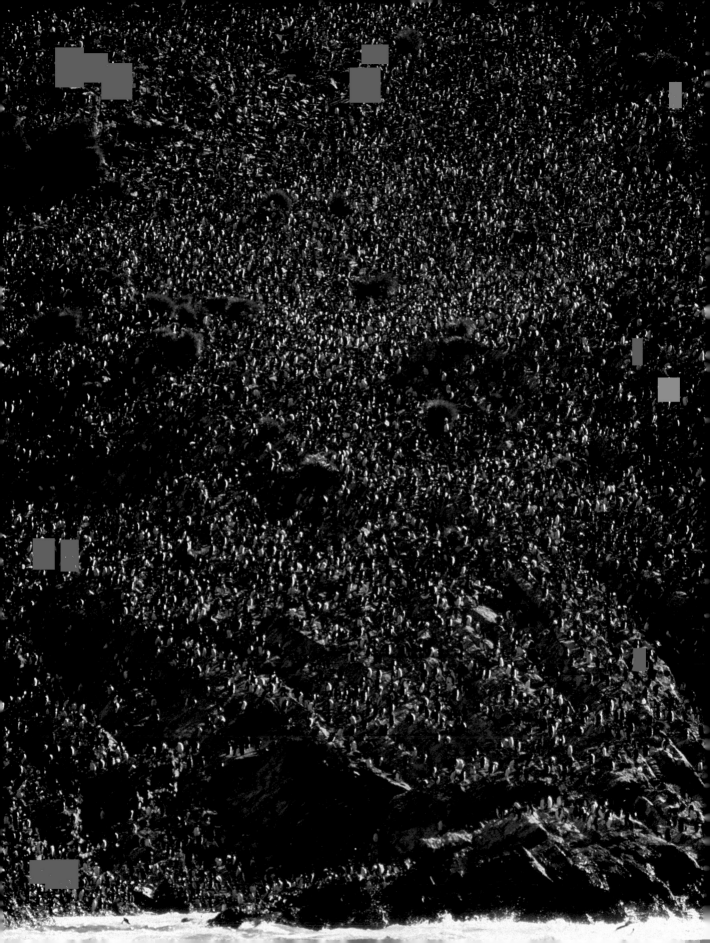

Death and Guano

In Antarctica there is no tussock grass. Nothing living or dead is hidden. Everything is visible. And in the concentrated colonies of thousands of penguins it is not only guano that accumulates, it is also the evidence of death. Death is everywhere. Naturally, all animals die sooner or later, but not all of them gather in the thousands in a climate where organic material does not rot very fast. In the Antarctic, whatever is not eaten by skuas or sheathbills remains, sometimes to be mummified. Skeletons and skins do not sink into water, are not consumed by beetles, are not covered by grass. They lie on the sand and rock as welcome mats to tourists in search of a natural idyll.

In the Antarctic it is not just the penguins that contribute to the sense of disarray, but they do their part. In his book on Alaska, *Coming into the Country*, John McPhee wrote that when you see someone in one of the lower forty-eight states whose yard is filled with several rusted hulks of cars, and an old washing machine, a few tubs, and assorted other junk, these are just Alaskans who haven't emigrated yet. Antarctica is Nature's version of the Alaskan's yard. Nelson Island, one of the South Shetland Islands off the Antarctic Peninsula, was my first landfall in the Antarctic, and my first sensation was the smell of fish and ammonia. Then came the bodies of seals, mostly living, one dead, scattered about the beach among penguins walking here and there, skuas flying overhead, and bits of bone everywhere. A skeleton of a bird lay next to a bit of rusty wire (a remnant of some human visitation), and numerous penguin craniums were scattered about, some in the sand, others in the penguin colony itself, partly buried in guano.

On Nelson Island the penguin colonies were small. My first real penguin city was the huge chinstrap penguin colony on Deception Island, also in the South Shetlands. When you first land, the colony is not visible. At first you see only a black sand beach, scoured by waves and traversed by lines of penguins walking in step, dirty ones toward the sea, clean ones back from the sea. The scene is graced by one touch of color, the salmon-pink underside of the penguins' flippers where blood is circulating near the surface to help the birds shed excess heat. The effect is subtle and charming.

And then, you turn a corner to find that once again, God has failed to restrain himself and has gone altogether too far. There, in the middle distance, are rolling hills of a pale pink, covered with infinitesimal black dots that turn out to be penguins—in the tens of thousands. The enormous hills are like a watercolor city of Oz, except that here the faded pastel is not an effect created in the mind of an Impressionist painter. It is, to be blunt, the color of shit. Of course, "penguin guano" is a more polite way to say it, but the impression it makes is not a polite one. In fact, primness and delicacy are thoroughly out of place in the penguin world. Because whatever you want to call this stuff, there are acres and acres and acres of it. And throughout this fantastic city of excrement are stained and noisy chinstrap penguins, skeletons, skuas eating bloody carcasses, penguins pecking each other, penguins squawking raucous and gull-like, hopping, trying to run, ducking the blows of other penguins, and regurgitating food for their young. Here are acres and acres of gaping beaks, of birds falling down on the pastel turf, of penguins shouting about things of tremendous importance to them, but a mystery to us. Here are birds in numbers such that they don't seem like birds at all, but more like some kind of cultivated plant crop sprouting up and down the fertilized hillsides—vast rolling fields of penguins.

Penguin cities are so large, their citizens so ill-mannered, and their pathways so difficult to traverse, that all of the penguins who live in them have developed something called the *slender walk* that they use to get them through the crowds alive. It varies from species to species, but in all the birds it is an attempt to appear as unthreatening as possible. Flippers back or sometimes all the way forward, head usually up but in some species down, body stance as slim as possible, the birds try to thread their way to the sea or back to their nests without sustaining bodily injury. They are reminiscent of New York City subway riders trying to get out of packed rush-hour cars, muttering, "Excuse me, getting out, getting out, excuse me," all the while keeping an eye out for muggers and lunatics—in other words, the other ten or forty thousand penguins.

OVERLEAF: *Rock hoppers and black-browed albatrosses nest together in a cliffside colony in the Falkland Islands. When the birds nest in such concentration and such numbers, the colonies can be smelled before they are seen.*

For those who prefer their animals manicured and popularized—Disneyized—real penguins are not easy to come to terms with. On the first meeting between naive penguin lover and real penguin, the little man in evening clothes dies a quick death. It has been said that familiarity breeds contempt. I would not say that this is true of penguins. (Of geese, perhaps, but not penguins.) Familiarity with penguins may breed, in the squeamish, momentary distaste, even revulsion, and certainly some puzzlement as to how these creatures can be so cute in theory and so nasty in practice. In the more robust sensibility, familiarity with penguins may breed open-mouthed (but usually closed-nosed) astonishment, wonder, admiration. But not contempt. Real penguins have too much grit. They defy scorn. They thrive in incomprehensible abundance in environments so harsh that the noise and odor of the birds become, after a while, welcome. In the Antarctic the penguins bring life to the rocks and ice. To be sure, there is far more Henry Miller than Walt Disney in the lives of penguins. But then, there is far more Henry Miller than Walt Disney in all our lives.

Asked to describe the magellanic penguin, Dee Boersma, who studies this bird in the hundreds of thousands at Punta Tombo in Argentina, said, "I guess I'd describe it as determined and feisty. I mean they just don't take anything from anybody, which is one of the reasons why I find them so enjoyable." That description holds for the other penguins as well, and it is a real, unsentimental reason to hold penguins in high regard, one that will not lead to disappointment in the face of the birds themselves.

What Are Penguins?

That said, a number of questions remain. Beyond the white tie and tails, beyond the initial blast of noise and smell, what are penguins really like? Beyond being

---

LEFT: *An Adélie penguin colony at Paulet Island, off the Antarctic Peninsula, shows not only the number of birds and the even spacing of their nests, but their effect on the landscape. The salmon color under them is not the tone of earth or rock, but of a thick coat of guano.*

OVERLEAF: *Gentoo penguins en masse and on the march. Gentoos tend to nest in smaller groupings than the Adélies or rock hoppers, but like most penguins, they have a need for togetherness.*

determined and feisty, which they certainly are, what kind of birds are penguins?

Much of the answer depends on the species. But there are characteristics, general qualities, that we can put together that say *penguin*. And Watson's description is as good a place to start as any: "Penguins are stocky flightless highly aquatic birds with dark upperparts and white underparts." We have considered at length the issue of the upperparts and underparts. Let's begin with *stocky*. Penguins are indeed stocky. They range in height, standing upright, from the very small little blue penguin of Australia, at sixteen inches high, to the four-foot-tall emperor. They range in weight from an average of two-and-a-half pounds for the little blue penguin to an average of sixty-some-odd pounds for the emperor, and from as little as one-and-a-half pounds to one hundred pounds. And they have not

ABOVE: *A king penguin colony on South Georgia Island. The Antarctic explorer Edward Wilson visited a similar congregation and noted, "All was stinking mud and in this wet filth the King Penguins were living and breeding."*

only weight but sturdiness. They are built like short, fat torpedoes with feet stuck on the bottom as an afterthought.

They are diving, not flying birds, and their bones are heavy, not light; solid, not hollow like those of flying birds. They are well muscled for swimming and well insulated with fat. There is one extinct penguin that is estimated, on the basis of a foot bone, to have been well over five feet tall, perhaps even as much as five feet seven. George Gaylord Simpson, describing it, wrote, "If *Anthropornis norden-skjoeldi* had a standing height of 5 feet 4 inches, which is quite likely, it probably weighed around 300 pounds when reasonably well nourished. As penguins in general are not timid toward humans, a large man would have done well to avoid one of those birds—but there were no men around."

The men were absent because penguins first evolved at least 45 million years ago. And the fossil evidence for *Anthropornis nordenskjoeldi*, discovered on Seymour Island in the Antarctic, indicates that this particular penguin had disappeared by about 37 million years ago. Not only weren't there any human beings in the Antarctic then, there weren't any human beings at all. The first primates that walked upright that we know of appeared about three-and-a-half million years ago. It wasn't until about forty thousand years ago that modern human beings replaced the Neanderthals and began the process of population growth and global expansion that would one day bring us to the Antarctic to chuckle over, and fry in butter when we were hungry, the little men in evening clothes.

As to the power of penguins, one need not look to the extinct sort. There is an account, in Robert Scott's *The Voyage of the* Discovery, of an encounter between men and emperor penguins that reflects positively on the emperors' abilities. As to what it says about the men, I'll let it speak for itself. Scott here is quoting from his own diary entry:

> On the night of the 8th there was a great Emperor penguin hunt....It is no easy matter to hold an Emperor; they are extraordinarily strong both in their legs and flippers, and are capable of moving even with a man on top of them. They could of course have been clubbed, but that would have damaged them as specimens. The proper method was to get hold of them firmly and give the

 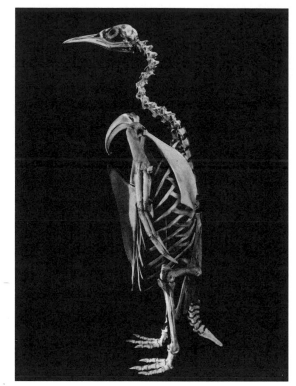

coup de grace in a scientific manner by inserting the blade of a penknife at the base of the skull. The confusion in the dark, when everyone was trying to capture a bird and these powerful creatures were dashing in every direction, can better be imagined than described. Report says that frequently one man was trying to capture another under the impression that he was a penguin, and more than one of the party seem to have been temporarily floored by the wild dashes of the intended victims. It was late at night before sufficient specimens had been slain, and then the party returned with a plentiful supply of frost-bites, of which they had been quite oblivious in the excitement of the chase.

Scott adds that although "the above scene may sound somewhat bloodthirsty," they only killed the penguins they needed, for food or for specimens.

ABOVE: *An emperor penguin and its skeleton. Like all penguins, the emperor is built something like a fat torpedo. Its waddling walk is a result of having its feet under it, where they don't interrupt the clean lines of the bird in the water.*

Robert Cushman Murphy offers another account that suggests "the great strength and vitality of a lusty Emperor Penguin." He writes,

> Five men from the Dundee whaler *Balaena* tried to overcome an Emperor Penguin without harming it, and to hold it down on the ice. They were quite unequal to the task and were bowled about like ninepins. Eventually they succeeded in strapping two leather belts around the bird's body, and, standing back, they took a breath. So did the penguin, and burst the belts. The capable creature was finally secured with a rope, but when hoisted on board it knocked out the ship's dog with a blow of its flipper.

This great and powerful beast weighed a total of seventy-four pounds. So. Stocky. Also sturdy, and strong. We must keep in mind, after all, that these were not ornithologists trying to restrain this bird. These were whalers, men presumably used to physical struggle.

Next comes "flightless" and "highly aquatic," which go together in the case of penguins. I have spoken to well-educated people who have expressed some doubt as to whether penguins are birds. This is not as silly as it may sound. Penguins may spend half of every year at sea. Many of the birds spend all the time they are not nesting either at sea or on ice floes. The penguins are descended from birds that did fly, probably birds like the diving petrels, or the auks of the Northern Hemisphere. These are birds that fly poorly but swim well, and not with their feet, as ducks do. They use their wings, which are a compromise between the requirements of two media: air and water. What happened in the case of penguins is that they evolved past the point of compromise. The lives of penguins at sea, and their adaptations to the water, are the subjects of a later chapter. But for the moment, we can say that anyone who has seen the birds in the water will agree that the sea is their true home.

That, then, is the generic penguin. A solid, determined, sharp-billed, and as often as not, phlegmatic bird on land (a few are quite shy), that spends most of its life

---

OVERLEAF: *King penguin feathers on the ground. Penguins molt, losing all their feathers and growing new ones, once a year. They do this on land, since a full coat of feathers is needed for waterproofing and insulation in cold seas.*

away from our view, in the water. But this is only the merest glimpse of penguins. They are not at all slaves to conformity. Well, actually they are, at least as individuals in a breeding colony. The foundation of the colonial penguin's way of life is conformity. A bird strives to arrive, mate, and leave just when all the other penguins do. But as *species* rather than individuals, penguins show considerable variation in their size, coloration, and in the sort of environment in which they live.

Penguins live all over the Southern Hemisphere in a great many different sorts of landscapes. No single image adequately represents all the penguins, certainly not that of the Adélie or the emperor waddling on ice with glaciers in the background. We also need to imagine penguins in tall grass. Penguins in burrows. Tiny penguins. Nocturnal penguins. Solitary penguins that nest in forests and are quiet and secretive. Even penguins nesting, on occasion, in the very low branches of trees on the Snares Islands off New Zealand. The penguins of the Antarctic are, in fact, no more characteristic of penguin life on average than the penguins of the Galápagos, which live at the equator.

Indeed, a tour through the varieties of penguins is a tour through the shores of the Southern Hemisphere. In taxonomic terms, the penguins are a family. Within the family are six genera, and, by some counts, eighteen species. They range from the Galápagos down the western coast of South America around Cape Horn and up the Patagonian coast. There are penguins all around the tip of South Africa. There are penguins in Australia and New Zealand, and there are absolute mobs of penguins in the subantarctic islands below New Zealand.

Throughout the Southern Ocean, the circumpolar body of water that circles the Antarctic Continent, and in the far southern Atlantic and Indian oceans, wherever there are islands, there are penguins. The names of these islands are unfamiliar to most of us, but to those who have traveled in the Southern Ocean they call to mind beaches and cliffs that are home to seabirds, seals, and penguins in the millions. Diego Ramírez and Staten off the tip of South America, the Falklands and South Georgia, Gough and Tristan da Cunha in the South Atlantic, Bouvet Island, and the

PRECEDING OVERLEAF: *A colony of king penguins. The rich color pattern of the adults is interwoven with the monochromatic brown of chicks still in their original down.*

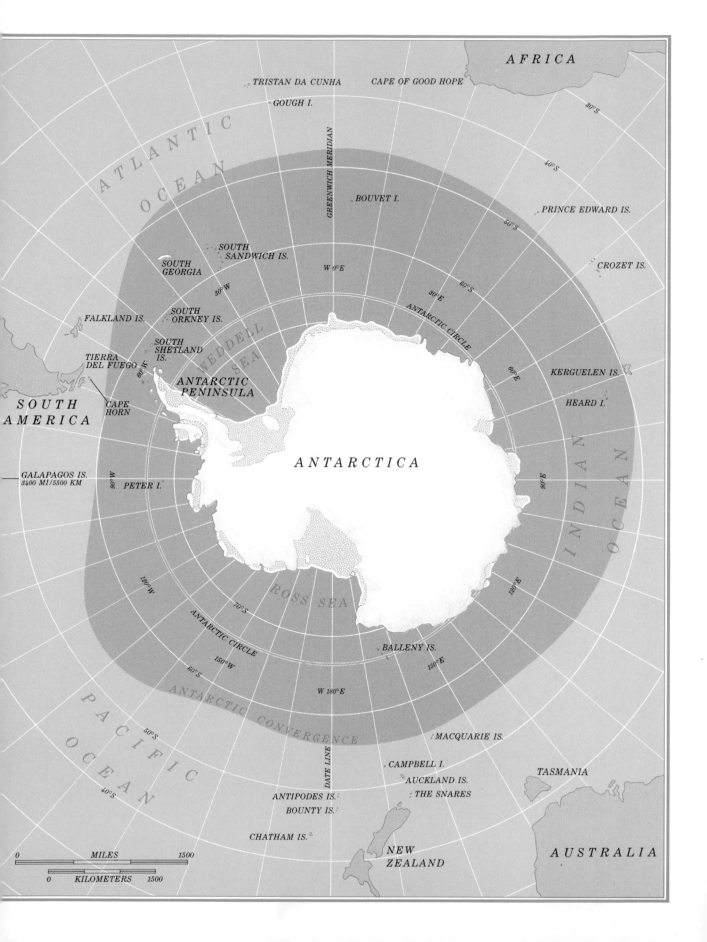

King

Emperor

Rock hopper

Fjordland crested

White-flippered

Little Blue

Snares Island

Erect-crested

Yellow-eyed

Chinstrap

Adélie

Gentoo

Macaroni

Royal

Black-footed

Peruvian

Magellanic

Galápagos

Prince Edward Islands south of Africa, the Crozets and Kerguelen in the Southern Indian Ocean, and Macquarie, the Snares, and others off New Zealand. Off the Antarctic Peninsula there are the South Shetlands, the South Orkneys, and the South Sandwich islands. There is the Antarctic Peninsula itself. And then, within the Antarctic Circle, in the coldest environment of all, on the continent and its floating ice shelves, we find the best-known penguins of all, the Adélies and the emperors.

The Penguins' World

There are two useful boundaries in talking about the Antarctic and environs. One, the less significant, is the Antarctic Circle, an artificial boundary at $66\frac{1}{2}$ degrees south latitude. It is not exactly imaginary, but what it marks has to do not with climate or animal life, but with the heavens. This is the boundary of the midnight sun and the dark days of winter. Below this line the sun cannot be seen during the Austral winter (although some light may creep over the horizon) and never completely disappears during the Austral summer.

The other, a climatic boundary, is the Antarctic Convergence, which marks off what is sometimes called the Southern Ocean (although this may be used to describe the whole of the unbroken ocean surrounding the Antarctic Continent) or the Antarctic Ocean. The Convergence is a changing line between 49 and 62 degrees south latitude where cold southerly ocean water turns under the surface and down to the sea floor to return to the Antarctic Continent. At the Convergence there is a change in temperature of the surface water of two degrees within a half degree of latitude. On a ship the Convergence can sometimes be recognized by fogs and mists, and by hordes of seabirds feeding off krill that have been killed by the shifting temperature boundary. In general, the Antarctic is the area below the Convergence. There are other boundaries pertinent to penguins, but these are the most important.

The emperor penguin, *Aptenodytes forsteri,* is the biggest penguin, the deepest diver, and the one that lives farthest south, far below the Antarctic Convergence and well within the Antarctic Circle. The classic image of the emperor is of birds standing alone or huddled together in the Antarctic winter, unmoving as the temperature reaches -60°F or -70°F. The birds have only a trace of orange color in their neck patches, in contrast to the rich color of the kings, the only other members of

the genus. Of all the penguins the emperor has the most appealing chick, with its gray, fuzzy, baggy body topped by a black cape, large white circles around the eyes and cheeks, and black eyes.

These are the most impressive of the penguins. Standing still, surrounded by ice and mountains, they may suggest visiting wise men or extraterrestrials. Of course, their apparent serenity (that is, when undisturbed; when upset they are as capable of making a racket as any other penguin) is probably an adaptation to the cold. The less one moves, the less energy one uses up. The emperor has several other cold-weather adaptations. One is its size. The bigger the bird, the less surface area in relation to volume, and consequently the less heat loss. Furthermore, the emperor is very heavily insulated. It has a thick layer of fat, and its feathers extend down onto its feet and onto its beak. (Only the Adélie, also a very southern bird, and smaller, is more heavily feathered.)

ABOVE: *The Castle Berg. This photograph was taken by Herbert G. Ponting, one of the first Antarctic photographers.*

Its behavior is also suited to the cold. The emperor, contrary to what its name implies, is not at all standoffish. In fact, it is the least territorial of penguins. Emperor penguins do not peck each other for getting too close. In several other penguin species the chicks huddle together in crèches when the weather is bad, but not the adults, because such close proximity would not be tolerable. Among the emperors, when the weather gets cold enough, a group of adult males, all with eggs on their feet (they make no nests) will shuffle together and make something looking like a scrum in rugby. It is tempting to see the emperors as being something like the proverbial New Yorkers who, in a crisis, will stick together to keep up their spirits (or in the penguins' case, their temperature). Of course, as the fabric of New York City unravels, sticking together has given way to other, less cooperative, behaviors—looting, for example. Emperor society is in better shape, perhaps because of the very great incentive life in the far, far south provides. Where the emperors live, there is a permanent power failure.

There is one other penguin in this genus, the king: *Aptenodytes patagonica.* Three feet tall and slim, the king may weigh thirty to forty pounds. It was identified by the naturalist John Forster when he landed with Captain James Cook on South Georgia in 1775. (Much later, when the emperors were identified, Forster was honored in the Latin name of that species, *Aptenodytes forsteri.*) The emperors occupy the icy south, and the kings breed on cold temperate and subantarctic islands—South Georgia, Heard, Kerguélen, Macquarie, and others. Kings have also been found on Tierra del Fuego, at the tip of South America, but never farther north, in Patagonia, as the name suggests. Like the emperor, the king incubates its single egg on its feet, covered by a flap of skin, and the birds can be seen scrunched up like hunchbacked wizards staring off into the distance, keeping their eggs warm. Unlike the emperors, each bird has its nesting territory, and they do fight and squabble. They will bat each other with flippers and peck each other with their beaks, sometimes drawing blood. These are the birds used in the Diet Coke commercial I mentioned earlier, during the filming of which they pecked at, and shattered, numerous different plastic trays that had been strapped to them. In other words, it's no wonder they draw blood. A peck from a king penguin is not to be taken lightly.

The other penguins that share the Antarctic Continent and the islands just off the Antarctic Peninsula with the emperor are mostly of one genus. These are the pygoscelid, or brush-tailed penguins: the Adélie (*Pygoscelis adeliae*), about thirty inches tall, weighing from six to fourteen pounds, depending on the season and the individual bird; the chinstrap (*Pygoscelis antarctica*), also about thirty inches tall and weighing about nine pounds; and the gentoo, (*Pygoscelis papua*), again thirty inches in height and weighing from nine to thirteen pounds.

The names of penguins are usually straightforward. *Pygoscelis antarctica* is obvious. *Pygoscelis adeliae* derives its name, by way of the French Antarctic territory, *Terre Adélie*, from the wife of one of the great Antarctic explorers, Jule-Sebastian-Cesar Dumont d'Urville. But the gentoo is another story altogether. Sealers called it the "Johnny penguin" or "John penguin." In that incarnation, it seems to have given its name to the striated caracara, a bird of prey that feeds on young gentoo penguins in the Falklands and is called the "Johnny rook."

Forster, Cook's naturalist, is the one who gave the gentoo its Latin name. He seems to have named the bird after Papua, New Guinea, even though the specimens he was describing came from the Falkland Islands. He apparently gave credence to an earlier report that the gentoo had been found in New Guinea. It had not. There are no penguins of any sort in New Guinea. The word *gentoo* is even more difficult to trace. It is an archaic term meaning "a Hindu," or "Telugu," one of the peoples of India. George Gaylord Simpson guessed that perhaps the white mark on the gentoo's head reminded Falklanders of turbaned natives of India. Murphy earlier said, "I have been unable to trace the history of the name 'Gentoo,' which is current at the Falklands."

Among the brush-tailed penguins (they really do have brushy tails, which they use sometimes to sweep melt water away from the nest), the Adélies range the farthest south, living on the continental shores around the Antarctic (sometimes sharing land with the emperors), all the way up the Antarctic Peninsula, where the emperor does not breed, and on numerous Antarctic islands. The chinstraps live on the Antarctic Peninsula and the islands around Antarctica, not extending as far south as the Adélie, nor as far north as the gentoo. The latter bird, though it is

---

OVERLEAF: *Rock hopper penguins gather at the base of cliffs in the Falkland Islands. The birds enter and exit the sea where waves crash against the rocks.*

found on the Antarctic Peninsula, thrives in warmer, although not *warm*, climates, such as those of subantarctic islands.

All three brush-tailed penguins are circumpolar. They live on shores and islands all around the continent. They all lay two eggs and raise, usually, two chicks. The gentoo lives in small colonies and has a reasonably pacific nature. As to the other two birds: If the emperors, in their ability to huddle together in the face of adversity, bear some resemblance to ideal New Yorkers in a crisis, the chinstraps and Adélies are more typical urban creatures, citizens of the sort of penguin cities I described earlier.

The subject of nastiness in penguins is incomplete without considering the crested penguins. All six species of these penguins are in the genus *Eudyptes*; all are colonial and aggressive; all have garish, flyaway eyebrows of yellowish feathers. The macaroni (*Eudyptes chrysolophus*), about twenty-eight inches high, and the rock hopper (*Eudyptes chrysocome*), at twenty-five inches the smallest crested penguin, are both circumpolar; the others have more restricted ranges. The macaroni lives the farthest south of any of the crested penguins, even on the Antarctic Peninsula and on many Antarctic and subantarctic islands. It likes steep terrain and has a nasal, bleating rat-a-tat-tat call. It is solidly built, and has an almost military bearing, as if its eyebrows were the braid on a dress uniform. The one colony of macaronis I visited was so difficult to gain access to that numbers of tourists, and tour guides, were soaked in the landing process. The birds were unconcerned. They sat there calmly, displaying a certain smelly dignity.

The rock hopper is never dignified. Its range is farther north than that of the macaroni, on subantarctic islands. As for the others, the erect crested (*Eudyptes sclateri*, twenty-eight inches) and the fiordland crested (*Eudyptes pachyrynchus*, twenty to twenty-eight inches) breed on the subantarctic islands off New Zealand and on the New Zealand shores. The royal (*Eudyptes schlegeli*, twenty-seven to thirty inches), sometimes considered a subspecies of the macaroni, breeds on Macquarie Island south of New Zealand and a few others, and the Snares Island (*Eudyptes robustus*, twenty-nine inches), which is very similar to the fiordland, breeds only on the shores of its eponym, which lies south of New Zealand.

Some of these penguins live in bigger aggregations than the others. The erect crested penguins live in huge colonies with a noise and stench startling even to people who have visited other penguin cities. The fiordland crested penguins may nest in caves and under trees. The Snares Island birds, although their islands are more exposed, have been known to nest *in* the very low-lying branches of trees (touching the ground or close to it), according to Bernard Stonehouse. Although the crested penguins do, just barely, reach into the plain rocks of the Antarctic, they are creatures more often of lusher islands, where there is at least some vegetation, some grass, waving, like the penguins' tassels, in ocean winds.

The only other large group of penguins consists of the four species of banded penguins of the genus *Spheniscus*. Three of them are very similar. The magellanic penguins (*Spheniscus magellanicus*), named for Ferdinand Magellan, on whose circumnavigation they were first spotted by Europeans, range up and down the more southerly coasts of South America, as far north as 42 degrees latitude; the Humboldt or Peruvian penguins (*Spheniscus humboldti*) are found well up the west coast and also on the guano islands off Peru; the black-footed or jackass penguins (*Spheniscus demersus*) are found on the coast of South Africa and on islands off the coast. These three penguins are similar looking, with bands of black around a white throat; they nest in burrows or caves or under scrub trees or bushes; their average heights are in the mid- to upper-twenty-inch range; and they all make a similar sound. On the tip of South America, Cape Horn, I stood in a muddy penguin trail in tussock grass sometimes chin-high, seeing the odd penguin in the distance, smelling them everywhere, and marveling at how secretive and hidden they were. These were my first wild penguins, and they weren't at all what I had expected. They were more like muskrats on a bank, or prairie dogs standing by their holes. As soon as you approached one of them, if you could find your way to it on a trail through the grass, it would duck into its burrow.

As I stood listening to a seabird expert, Peter Harrison, talking about the birds around us, I was startled to hear a loud call come from within the high grass only a

OVERLEAF: *Following what to them is a well-worn path, the rock hoppers move up and down the cliffside, going to sea to feed and returning to climb up to their nests and feed their chicks.*

foot or so away. It began in a broken staccato and ended in the extended nasal sound of a small foghorn, something like a donkey imitating Woody Woodpecker. Harrison, hearing the call, said, "That of course is the magellanic, or jackass, penguin."

As a group these penguins have a common problem—the heat. Theirs is not the landscape of glaciers. Their habitat varies from the lava rocks of the Galápagos to Cape Horn (where the temperature is fine for penguins) to the hard dirt of the coastal islands off Africa. They all have less of their bodies feathered than the more southerly penguins. They show patches of bare skin on the face around the bill. The feathers do not extend as far down over the feet. They have less fat. And they burrow, getting away from predators and the sun. They burrow into the earth, and they burrow into accumulated, fossilized guano. They hide in caves and rock crevices in the Galápagos, and in holes dug in the earth on Cape Horn, the Cape of Good Hope, the Falklands, and at Punta Tombo in Argentina. Sometimes they simply nest under bushes.

These are the penguins that are closest and most accessible to people. At Punta Tombo, on a sparsely vegetated beach in a region that is almost a cold desert, there are about 200,000 breeding pairs. Many estimates run higher, but Dee Boersma, who studies the birds, says that the larger numbers, although they draw tourists, are not correct. It's easy enough for tourists to get there. Punta Tombo is within one hundred kilometers of the Argentine city of Trelew, with a population of more than 40,000 (people).

"You can't believe it," Boersma says of the site of birds densely packed on the beach. "It's definitely a spectacle of nature. In my view it rivals things that you see on the Serengeti." Boersma, incidentally, has what might be called, in scientific terms, "hard evidence" of the feistiness of penguins. All the spheniscid penguins, which are fish eaters, have a hooked bill to help them grab their prey. And the hook is sharp. Boersma has banded 32,000 penguins over the years, pulling them out from their burrows with a sort of shepherd's crook and then getting a hold on them. Of course, sometimes the reverse occurs. "I have several scars to show where the penguin has been more successful in the encounter than I have."

On the Falklands the magellanic penguins provide a spectacle of another sort. Here the penguins are found in sheep pastures. They make their burrows in terrain that is reminiscent of the west of Ireland, with rocky hills and pastures, and gray, cold skies—in the summer. The native tussock grass was burned down to grow fields of English grass for sheep, and burrows dot the pasture like gopher holes.

This genus includes the world's warmest-weather penguin, the Galápagos (*Spheniscus mendiculus*), also with a black band at its neck; it stands about twenty inches high. The Galápagos is one of the rarest penguins, with about 2,000 to 6,000 remaining. It is the absolute furthest in penguin physiology from the emperor. It weighs five-and-a-half pounds to the emperor's fifty or even one hundred pounds, has quite significant bare patches to shed heat, and nests in caves and crevices to hide from the sun. Iguanas, boobies, and frigate birds are its companions.

It is not, however, the smallest or, indeed, the strangest penguin, bearing in mind, of course, that *strange* is not exactly a scientific term, not in this context anyway. On Australia and New Zealand lives the smallest penguin of all, the little blue or fairy penguin (*Eudyptula minor*) and a subspecies, the white-flippered penguin. (Call it *Eudyptula albosignata* and you have eighteen species.) This bird lives in burrows, in small colonies on the coasts and islands of New Zealand and southern Australia. It is only sixteen inches high and weighs three pounds or less. Among the hazards it faces are not only dogs and ferrets, but the automobile. It is probably the only penguin that has tourists camped out, at night, with no parkas on, sitting on benches (this penguin lives in resort areas) to watch it parade from the sea across the beach to its home, as if, just to provide comic relief from an already comic family, somebody had invented a little wind-up species, perfect in all particulars.

The last species of penguin deserves some special note. It is the yellow-eyed penguin (*Megadyptes antipodes*, about thirty inches), also know as a YEP or Chookie. It lives in the forest on South Island, New Zealand, and on a few outlying islands, and it is the only penguin that is truly noncolonial. It doesn't gather in groups at all; rather, it sneaks off in pairs, into the forests. It is secretive and shy, not excessively noisy or ill-tempered. And it doesn't create a terrible smell.

The yellow-eyed penguin may seem like the most exotic of all the penguins, and perhaps the least known to North Americans, but it is a penguin that was studied with great thoroughness by Lance Richdale, a scientist with a taste for language. (His classic study was published in 1957.) He did not shy away from anthropomorphism. He described one behavior of the rock hopper penguin, for example, as a "sneering attitude."

Unlike its fellows in the Antarctic, where penguins are thriving, the yellow-eyed penguin is suffering. Its habitat of primitive conifer forests is disappearing on the coasts of South Island, New Zealand. And it faces dangers—mostly to the eggs and young—from ferrets, stoats, and cats. Interestingly, the dangers of the yellow-eyed penguin are not solely the result of western Europeans and their colonizing activities. In this case the Polynesians are the first to blame. There were no mammalian predators on New Zealand until the Polynesians arrived about 800 years ago, bringing with them (inadvertently, of course) *Rattus exulans*, the Polynesian rat. Of course, more recently, more, and more effective, predators have been introduced and the bird's favored forests cut down. In some grassland areas, according to a recent study by John Darby of the University of New Zealand, *all* the chicks are killed within four weeks of hatching.

It may be worth noting, as an aside to this gallery of penguin species, that the paleontologist George Gaylord Simpson, one of this century's prominent evolutionary theorists, and a devotee of penguins, wrote a wonderful book, *Penguins: Past and Present, Here and There*. In it, he gives a section over to the naming of penguins, in which he makes a plea that the yellow-eyed penguin and little blue penguin be called by their Maori names, respectively, *hoiho* and *kororaa*. Among the other names given penguins by the Maoris are *Tauake* for the fiordland, and *tawaki* and *pokotiwha* for the rock hopper. The Peruvian penguin and the magellanic penguin were named by the Indians who lived near them, and those names are

---

ABOVE: *A group of Humboldt, or Peruvian, penguins at the New York Zoological Society's Bronx Zoo. These penguins, often seen in zoos, are in trouble in the wild.*

petranca and *choncha*, respectively. There must have been an African name or names for the black-footed penguin, but I haven't found it.

As for the other penguins, they entered language and taxonomy when they encountered European sailors, explorers, and scientists. Indeed, the very name *penguin* seems, by all accounts, to have been first applied not to what we think of as penguins, but to the now extinct great auk or garefowl, the largest of the auks, a bird exclusively of the northern seas. Like the penguins of the Southern Hemisphere it was a stocky, flightless, highly aquatic bird with dark upperparts and white underparts. It was in decline for many years before it finally went extinct, but its species is one of the few for which we know the particulars of the end. According to Simpson, the last two great auks in the world were shot and killed in the course of a routine hunt by Sigurder Islefsson and Jon Brandsson of Iceland on June 4, 1844.

OVERLEAF: *Rock hopper penguins on the march on flatter ground. The rock hoppers do not live in the extreme cold of the Antarctic Continent itself but are found on islands all around the Southern Ocean.*

PAGES **100-101**: *Tussock grass, through which penguins make paths, and in which they may nest, once covered much of the Falkland Islands. (Most of it was burned off to make pasture for sheep by settlers.)*

3 Do You Want to Dance?

> SHE MAY STOP AND RESPOND WITH THE "OBLIQUE STARE BOW": THE HEAD IS LOWERED SLOWLY AND TURNED SIDE-WAYS. THE MALE ALSO MAY PERFORM THE OBLIQUE STARE BOW VIS-À-VIS A STRANGE FEMALE. IT IS THE OPPOSITE OF ATTACK …
> —Dietland Müller-Schwarze, *The Behavior of Penguins*, 1984

Among the many pleasures of natural history, sex—in the broad sense of the word, encompassing courtship, mating, and reproduction—is foremost. It is a foundation of animal society. It is the force that through the green fuse drives the flower and through the red fuse grows antlers and fancy tail feathers. It is a primary source of ritual and display. Penguin cities are built on sex. The reason the birds gather on land in the first place is to reproduce, and almost everything they do there is connected, directly or indirectly, to this end. Other than egg laying and hatching and chick raising, penguins have precious little reason to come on land at all. They do need to leave the water to molt once a year, but that's a solitary pursuit that doesn't require conversation, visual or vocal.

In the matter of mating display and ritual, penguins do have some limitations. They do not have breeding plumage, for instance. Nor do they have melodious mating calls that fill the soul (the human soul, that is) with inspiration. Nonetheless, they do have stylized, dancelike courtships involving dips, bows, stares, curtsies, and calls, the exact composition of which is idiosyncratic to each species. The Adélies have the most elaborate behaviors, the little blue penguins the least. And the emperors, which mate in colder regions than any other bird on earth, in the gathering night of the Austral winter, have a subdued austerity to their courtship that suits their environment.

Here, from *Visual and Vocal Signals in Penguins, Their Evolution and Adaptive Characters* (1982), by Pierre Jouventin, a book not entirely without poetry, is an account of how penguin courtship begins:

RIGHT: *A king penguin in its ecstatic display. Flippers outstretched, bill pointed skyward, the bird gives forth a drawn-out, brassy, trumpeting sound.*

FOLLOWING PAGES: *Two macaroni penguins together in the tussock grass, and two king penguins in the midst of courtship.*

A bachelor Emperor penguin sings somewhere in the colony: it stops, lets
its head fall on its chest ... takes a big breath, utters its call with lowered
head, stands still for 1 or 2 s[econds] more, then continues its walk, repeat-
ing the behavior further on. The receptive female freezes, stretched as tall
as possible, and is imitated by its partner, the birds more or less facing each
other.... They slowly lift their heads while progressively contracting their
neck muscles, freeze in this position for several min[utes], then little by little relax and assume more normal attitudes.

At this point in the ritual the pair either stays together, continuing the courtship
until they mate and produce an egg, or separates, each to go look for other mates.
What they look for and why one penguin is less appealing than another are matters
for speculation. What is known is that if the two emperors stay together, they will
proceed to promenade together in the so-called waddling gait (presumably the waddle is even more pronounced than usual), the female following the male. Later in the
courtship, bowing commences, on the part of both birds, and copulation ensues.

Among penguins, as with most creatures, copulation itself is quickly done. In
penguins, the female lies down on her stomach and the male stands on her back. In
some species copulation is accompanied by bill rubbing or flipper flapping, but not
in the emperors. One seabird specialist says that in penguins the act of mating is a
bit like the male surfing on the female. Indeed, females can be picked out, during
breeding season, by the dirty footprints on their backs. I have seen one pair of penguins, chinstraps, in the act of mating. The female lay on her stomach. The male
hopped onto her back and stood there, trying to maintain his footing, while they
both rubbed their bills together until the climactic moment, after which the male
hopped off without further ado.

After copulation emperor penguins indulge in a behavior that may serve, as biol-
ogists like to say, to reinforce the pair bond. (One day I am going to send my wife a
Valentine's Day card that reads, "To Reinforce Our Pair Bond, Dear.") The birds,

---

LEFT: *Two magellanic penguins in a mutual display, a part of the mating ritual. These
birds make a braying sound, hence one colloquial name for them—jackass penguins.*

writes Jouventin, "sometimes stand chest to chest or lie flipper to flipper. Egg laying occurs amidst bows; once the egg is laid the first duets are heard."

It is the business of science to make observations of these behaviors, and sometimes to make judgments about their role in the task of reproduction. But science cannot say what the penguins experience. Even to discuss the consciousness of animals is scientifically controversial. Those of us not burdened by scientific expertise and reputation can, however, make any guesses we like. And my guess is this: Looked at from an evolutionary perspective, reproduction is so important for any animal, and cooperation in a penguin pair so necessary to raise chicks, that I think courtship and bonding must produce powerful positive feelings of some sort in penguins. We only have words for our own feelings, and it's highly risky to apply them

---

ABOVE: *A hungry, almost fully grown gentoo chick chases its parent, demanding to be fed. Penguin chicks sometimes almost run up the parent's back before the adult will stop and regurgitate food for the chick.*

to stocky, flightless seabirds, but my own version of mild anthropomorphism (animals *are* like people in some ways) makes me imagine that emperor penguins in postcopulatory closeness, standing chest to chest, or lying flipper to flipper must feel something akin to peace.

Waltzes and Waddles

Each penguin species has its own variant of this mating ritual. The Adélies have their oblique stare bows and other sophisticated mating-dance steps. The king penguins click their bills as they bow to each other, much the way wandering albatrosses do. They also have an "advertisement walk" or "waddling gait" similar to that of the emperors. Male kings (no, the female kings are not called queens) parade before females, one or more of whom will try to follow the male, sometimes fighting each other for the privilege. The spectacular orange neck markings play their part in this process. Bernard Stonehouse, a scientist once described to me by a colleague as Mr. Penguin, because of his extensive work, particularly with the kings, once tried painting over the neck spots of two males and found that they couldn't attract a female. One found no partner, and the other managed to mate only after the paint had flaked and fallen off.

The rock hoppers shake their heads as they give their ecstatic cry, as do the other crested penguins, making their eyebrow feathers fly, thus producing a "halo" effect. Among the jackass penguins, instead of the waddling gait of the emperors and kings there is something called an *automaton gait*. In some species (the ones in warmer climates that carry lice and other passengers), courting and mated birds preen each other. And after mating, when male and female are to change shifts, taking over incubation, or watching the chick, they go through rituals as well, bowing to each other, calling, singing duets.

They may not, however, give each other presents. One of the best-known courtship behaviors of the Adélie penguin seems to be in some doubt. Certainly, after mating, the birds, in particular the male, gather stones for the nest. But as to the offering of pebbles as part of the courtship, Jouventin says, "the behavior is too inefficient to be nest-building and too infrequent to be a display." He calls it a "displacement activity," which, to get scientific about it, is an irrelevant movement that

occurs in a conflict situation. Anyone who doubts that courtship is a conflict situation has forgotten his or her adolescence. I take this interpretation of pebble giving to mean that it is something like a shy boy shuffling his feet or looking off into space in the presence of the girl he wants to kiss. The behavior may occur often during courtship, but it's not part of the display that moves the relationship forward.

In all the penguins, with all their bows and stares, one behavior is paramount. It is the ecstatic display, or Ecstatic Vocalization—sometimes shortened to EV. It is used not only to attract mates but also to announce territory, or simply to announce oneself. When walking through a penguin colony, anyone can spot a penguin in ecstasy. In all but two species (the emperor, which puts its head down, and the little penguin, which points its bill forward), the ecstatic display involves throwing the bill skyward. The flippers are stretched back, or out, or forward, or down, and the

ABOVE: *Two chinstraps in the act of mating, which is accompanied by much clicking together of bills. During mating season, the females are often seen with dirty footprints on their backs.*

bird utters whatever sound it has been endowed with—the elegant, brassy notes of the king penguin, the squawks, barks, and Arks! of Adélies, chinstraps, and rock hoppers, or the brayings of the jackass penguins. When two penguins together each give forth with something similar to an ecstatic cry, they are indulging in a mutual display, or a Loud Mutual Vocalization (LMV).

EVs and LMVs may sound as if they have more to do with lunar landings than love among birds. And the tone of these terms reflects a progression (although perhaps not progress) in the language of science. Edward Wilson first used the term "ecstatic display" in 1907, and it reflects his comfort with the English language and his willingness to use a terminology rich in associations and connotation to describe the activities of birds. Scientists no longer like to be so loose. They seek precision and rigor, wishing to protect the language of science from miscegenation with the

---

ABOVE: *A male king penguin mounting a female. One seasoned (male) observer of penguins and their mating habits has suggested that mating, for the male, must be something like surfing. He did not suggest what it must be like for the female.*

sentimentally vulgar language the rest of us use. Sometimes, this makes sense. The ecstatic display actually has nothing to do with ecstasy. And no sensible scientist, no sensible person, really, wants to fall into the sort of wallow that was acceptable in Cherry Kearton's time, with Mr. and Mrs. Penguin all but whispering endearments to one another. On the other hand, I wonder whether an Ecstatic Vocalization is more precise then an ecstatic call or cry, and what great benefit is derived from cluttering up manuscripts with impressive capital letters—LMVs and the like. Brevity is not always the soul of wit, or science.

Of course, even scientific prose has its moments. Consider the following passage from *Breeding Biology of the Adélie Penguin* by David G. Ainley, Robert E. LeResche, and William J. Sladen. The authors write that on arriving at the nesting ground and staking out a nest territory, the Adélie indulges in two calls, one of

ABOVE: *A gentoo penguin sitting on a nest of rocks and pebbles incubates its eggs. Most penguins lay two eggs, and males and females share in incubating the eggs and raising the chicks.*

which is the EV and the other the Locomotory Hesitancy Vocalization (LHV). They go on to assert that both displays "are highly individualistic and are largely proclamations of self: 'This is me, Adélie Penguin X, and I am approaching (LHV) or occupying (EV) my space, my territory.'" The statement strikes me as remarkably similar in content, if not in tone, to the line in e.e. cummings's poem about the kingbird: "his royal warcry is I AM."

Penguins are particularly attractive to ethologists (the scientists who study the behavior of animals in the wild). The colonial species, at least, concentrate themselves for easy observation and are unafraid of human observers. There is no need to erect blinds or wear camouflage. The birds are easily watched and relatively easily captured (relative to a Bengal tiger, say, or a killer whale) and banded for later identification. The banding helps observers go beyond deciphering mating dances,

ABOVE: *A magellanic penguin at the mouth of the burrow where it makes its nest. In high tussock grass magellanic penguins, all with underground nests, can be heard and smelled more easily than they can be seen.*

which, after all, are only one part of penguin behavior. With banding, a scientist can track the life histories of individual penguins. Furthermore, using the banded penguins as a sample group, much the way Gallup does when he conducts a poll, scientists can follow the activity of a colony as a whole—not an easy task.

Nesting colonies are made up not only of penguin families but of single birds that seem to be at loose ends. They are either too young, or too late in arriving, or have lost mates, or are just practicing mating behavior, getting ready for next year. Other birds switch mates or lose them during the breeding season. Among these apparently extraneous birds, in Adélies, at any rate, are ones known as *wanderers*. They do just that, moving in and around colonies, sometimes wandering off to another colony. Most of these are young birds. Some of their movements are desultory and not terrifically energetic. Others are, as Ainley and his coauthors put it, "more impressive." One bird covered 74 kilometers in a day. Sometimes these young birds behave badly, bothering the established families, resulting in their being termed *hooligans*. The term reflects the observer's point of view, but I would be willing to bet that in this instance, penguin and human perceptions coincide.

Even among mated birds, the standardized course of display, mating, and then raising the chicks with the mate does not always go the way it is supposed to. Take the case of female 519-17485. She "bred with one male (A) as a three-year-old, kept company with a second male as a four-year-old, and bred with a third male (B) as a five-year-old." As a six-year-old she started out with male C, but in less than a week switched to a different nest site. She was seen there alone while male C was on his nest with another bird. (The males stake out the nest sites.) Two days later she moved on to male D and a third nest. The next day she moved back to male C and his nest, where she laid an egg. That egg was lost in a storm, and she then disappeared for two weeks, apparently going to sea. She returned to male C's nest where she incubated two eggs laid by another female that had been on the nest during her absence. She hatched these two eggs and raised one chick to fledging. And, say the authors, "All the while, this female's mate from the previous year bred one meter away."

For anyone who imagines (as I often do) nature as an ideal state, who suspects that if only we had fewer credit cards and less self-awareness, if only our brains were smaller and our mating rituals simpler, life would move along so much more smoothly, female 519-17485 provides a powerful dose of reality. Indeed, that seems to me one of the main values of ethology (of all science, if you think about it): the information it uncovers, if we care to examine it, forces us to confront nature as it is, not as we might like to imagine it.

Breaking the Pair Bond

Among the mistaken notions many people have of penguins is that they mate for life. We think of penguins forming pair bonds that last for years. We may be tempted to imagine their bonds as something like our marriages—Mr. and Mrs. Penguin. Well, yes and no. They're certainly not promiscuous. Like most long-lived seabirds, penguins do form attachments to both nests and mates, and though these attachments vary from species to species, most penguins would probably be described as monogamous to one degree or another. But look at the emperors. One study shows only 14 percent staying with the same mate from one year to the next. Adélies have been considered among the most faithful, but their behavior varies. In some colonies, 80 percent of the birds stick with the same mate from year to year. But in the very southern Cape Crozier colony studied by Ainley, fidelity in a given year is usually around 50 percent. In the research Ainley and his coauthors discuss in their book, none of the banded birds under study kept the same mate for more than four years. He writes, "No birds paired in 1969–1970 were still paired in 1974–1975."

The same was very nearly true for some human communities during that time period. But the reason for infidelity at Cape Crozier is not that the birds have roving eyes or midlife crises or that Antarctic penguin society experienced a sexual revolution. The cause is to be found in climate—to wit, cold winters and short summers. Adélies at Cape Crozier (where, incidentally, the notoriously unfaithful emperors also nest) are under tremendous pressure to mate, lay eggs, and fledge

OVERLEAF: *Macaroni penguins on their nests on a rocky hillside. The macaronis are bigger and heavier than the rock hoppers. With their bushy, garish eyebrows, they sometimes have the look of slightly demented colonels.*

chicks. They arrive in late October, at the earliest, and the chicks are fledged and gone by early February. Individual birds may not be there for this entire time. They may arrive late or leave early. Of that time, incubation takes a little more than a month, and the chicks don't fledge until they are fifty days old. There is little time for dalliance. A Cape Crozier Adélie's primary requirement in a mate is neither looks nor sex appeal, but what the scientists call *synchrony*. Presumably the sexiest thing one Cape Crozier Adélie could say to another would be, "Ready when you are."

The climate also affects other aspects of Adélie breeding. They make their nests from stones, as do the chinstraps, gentoos, and macaronis in the Antarctic. These sorts of nests drain well when the snows melt. (Male Adélies, who occupy the nest

---

ABOVE: *Gentoos nesting on South Georgia Island. Gentoos, which do not nest in giant colonies, but tend to gather in smaller groups, will build their nests of grass and vegetation rather than rocks, if they can.*

sites, will find last year's site when they return in the breeding season, even if it is buried by snow.) And besides, there's no grass to make a softer nest. Because the Adélies build their nests of small round stones, and because they return year after year to the same rookeries, the stones accumulate. Thus, the birds have changed the landscape in some big colonies, where centuries of collapsed nest pebbles form undulating ridges.

While the birds begin their mating and sit on their nests they may face severe storms and blizzards. The winds benefit them when they are on the move since the winds break up the ice and give them open water so that they can get to the rookery quickly, thus using their fat reserves to fuel breeding rather than travel. As an indication of how sturdy the birds are, Ainley and his coauthors wrote that "even winds of well over 100 mph have beneficial effects for Adélies; but when they reach 140

ABOVE: *A magellanic penguin on the Falkland Islands rests in the mouth of its nest. On open pasture, penguin burrows dot the land like gopher holes.*

mph penguins have difficulty maintaining their footing." I asked him if that meant they could stand up at lesser speeds. He said yes, at 100 mph they could. "They hunker down and seem to do okay." He said that for humans, crawling seems to be a better mode of travel once the winds start getting up to about 90 mph.

The Adélie's life, except for the extreme pressure of climate, is not unlike that of many of the other colonial penguins. As Ainley puts it,

> To breed successfully, an Adélie penguin must accomplish three major
> social tasks: secure and maintain a territory upon which to build a nest,
> develop a pair bond with an individual of the opposite sex so that eggs are
> laid in that nest, and with its mate coordinate the care of eggs and chicks.
> All of these tasks are accomplished by the exchange of information between
> the Adélie and its neighbors, mate and offspring.

I guess that sums up the life of a penguin on land. But there are considerable variations on this theme. The yellow-eyed penguins are not colonial at all and so need less communication with their neighbors. It's their mates that they need to coordinate activities with. They are not migratory, nor do they spend months at sea. Rather, they seem to return to land each night, even when they are not breeding. The Galápagos penguins have no breeding season whatsoever. They wait until conditions in the Cromwell Current near them produce an abundance of food fish, and then they mate and lay their eggs, taking advantage of the surfeit while it is available.

The king penguins on South Georgia are not migratory either, although they will spend weeks at sea. They follow a very odd three-year breeding cycle deciphered by Bernard Stonehouse. It takes the kings thirteen to fourteen months to raise a chick to fledging, so that it is ready to go to sea on its own. The birds lay their eggs from November to March, and the eggs take about two months to hatch. If a bird breeds early in one year, it breeds late the next, and in the third year, it is too late to hatch a chick that will live through the Austral winter. Stonehouse, however,

RIGHT: *Chinstrap penguins start their nesting season early. Here, on South Georgia Island, the birds are incubating their eggs on nests still surrounded by snow.*

believes this cycle may be a result of climate and that in places where the winter is less harsh than at South Georgia, the cycle might be different. The end result is that in a colony of king penguins on South Georgia there are, at almost any time, birds mating, birds incubating eggs, and chicks wearing down that is not like the fuzz of Adélies and emperors, but more like ragged fur.

Nesting habits vary as well. The kings and emperors keep their eggs on their feet. The southerly, Antarctic penguins use stones for nests, but gentoos on the Falklands and other islands further north make nests of grass and vegetation. The *Spheniscus* penguins burrow, or nest under bushes, or, on the Galápagos, in caves. Except for the kings and emperors, which lay only one egg, the other penguins lay two. The crested penguins lay two eggs but raise only one chick. The first egg is smaller than the second, sometimes only half the size. Sometimes both eggs hatch,

---

ABOVE: *A gentoo penguin in a contemplative moment on its nest. Once the chicks hatch, the parents will be taking turns going to sea to catch food for them.*

but then the smaller chick dies quickly. Peter Harrison, the seabird expert, described this as "obligatory sibling murder," which I think has a nice ring to it. Some reports have it that the birds will kick one egg out of the nest. If, however, something untoward happens to the large egg or chick and the smaller chick is alive, then this Clark Kent offspring takes over and, with the benefit of all the food, transforms itself into a literally full-fledged penguin.

Married, with Children

So far we have talked mostly about mating and the overall patterns of behavior in penguin colonies, not about the demands of parenthood. In all of the penguins, males and females share the incubating, and in all the penguins, this involves some

---

ABOVE: *Two macaroni penguins display at the nest. In penguins, ritual dances are not over when mating occurs. The birds also have stylized behaviors for the changing of parental guard at the nest.*

hardship. But in no bird is the incubation more difficult or remarkable than in the case of the emperor. It begins after the courtship in the darkness of May or June, as the egg is laid amid bowing and duets. Shortly thereafter the female, with much more bowing and singing, transfers the egg from her feet to the male's feet. If all goes well, it won't touch ice until it cracks open and the chick comes out. The male tucks it under a flap of skin, known as a *brood patch*, that covers it and keeps it warm, and then he more or less stands still for two months. When the weather gets very bad all the males huddle together in their own crèche, a formation called a *tortue*, or "turtle" in French, to conserve body heat. All the penguin's energy, all his reserves of fat, go to maintaining his own body temperature and keeping the egg warm. It has been calculated that a bird in the turtle formation will lose only half as much weight as a bird alone.

The male, from the beginning of breeding until the chick hatches and the female returns, fasts. At the same time he faces the task of keeping his temperature up. He may be without food for more than four months and lose up to half of his body weight. And, at the end of that time of starvation, if, when the chick hatches, the female has not yet returned with krill in her gullet, the male will produce a nutritious secretion from his digestive system and regurgitate it to give the chick something to tide it over. This secretion is called *penguin's milk*.

There are some who say that no other creature on earth is quite as cute as a baby emperor penguin. This may or may not be connected to the emperor's extreme parenting instinct. Emperors will steal eggs, incubate pieces of ice that only look like eggs, and "chick-nap" another bird's baby just to have something to raise. In their colonies emperors also have a sizable surplus of unmated penguins just waiting to snatch up a child. The reason for this behavior, for the intense desire to parent, probably has to do with temperature. When it drops to -70°F, the point is not whose chick or egg it is, but that if somebody doesn't warm it up quick, it's dead. The

---

LEFT: *An emperor penguin with its chick. The emperor males incubate a single egg in the dark Antarctic winter for two months, not eating and losing up to half of their body weight. When the chick hatches, if the female has not returned, the male regurgitates a nutritious secretion called* penguin's milk.

emperor penguin egg was the reason for one of the most remarkable journeys in Antarctic history, which has no shortage of remarkable journeys. This was a trip on foot, hauling sledges in the darkness of the Antarctic winter, in temperatures that reached -77.5°F. The men who made it traveled in the Ross Sea area, across the 65 miles from Cape Evans to Cape Crozier and back. The goal was to gain eggs of the emperor penguin, which it was thought might provide evidence of the evolution of feathers. This hope was based on a theory current at the time, but mistaken, that an embryo in its development recapitulates the evolutionary history of its species. Nor is it true, as the explorers believed, and as one of them wrote, that the emperor is "the most primitive bird in existence." Rather, it is very highly specialized.

Nonetheless, the explorers knew none of this, and three of them, all part of Robert Falcon Scott's last expedition to the Antarctic, set out in late June from

ABOVE: *Left, a gentoo chick, underestimating its size, strives to gain the safety and warmth of a protective parent. Right, the adult, stoic in the face of an impossible demand, provides what comfort it can.*

Scott's base at Cape Evans for a thirty-six-day round trip. Edward Wilson was the leader and he took with him Henry Robertson ("Birdie") Bowers, and Apsley Cherry-Garrard, who later wrote a book, *The Worst Journey in the World*, in which he aptly captured the nature of the trip: "It is extraordinary how often angels and fools do the same thing in this life, and I have never been able to settle which we were on this journey."

In the darkness and the cold their clothes froze each morning as they emerged from their tent, locking them in one position for the time they were outside. Their sleeping bags froze, so that they had to fight their way into them at night. When they reached the rookery, they lost their tent in a storm and thought death was near. At the end of the journey, Cherry-Garrard's sleeping bag weighed twenty-seven pounds more than it had at the beginning. Every extra ounce was sweat that had frozen into ice.

The three men did indeed reach what was at that time the only known colony of emperors in the world and return with three eggs. In the end, Cherry-Garrard had difficulty in getting the British Museum to accept these prizes, let alone study them. Neither Wilson nor Bowers returned to England. After their winter expedition, they joined Scott on the summer race for the South Pole and died with him on that fatal journey.

Cherry-Garrard's account of the colony of emperor penguins is necessarily brief. The three men made one visit only, and since they were endangered by the cold and wind, they could only take the eggs, kill several birds for food, and flee to the safety of the rock igloo they had constructed for shelter. Cherry-Garrard wrote that although they were seeing a marvel of the natural world, and had endured "indescribable effort and hardship," they "had but a moment to give."

> The disturbed Emperors made a tremendous row, trumpeting with their curious metallic voices. Their was no doubt they had eggs, for they tried to shuffle along the ground without losing them off their feet. But when they were hustled a good many eggs were dropped and left lying on the ice, and some of these were quickly picked up by eggless Emperors who had probably been waiting a long time for the opportunity.

He goes on to write of the birds' behavior with chicks, which had been noted by an earlier expedition that visited the colony later in the season. He describes a male emperor guarding his chick:

> And they found him holding his precious chick balanced upon his big feet, and pressing it maternally or paternally (for both sexes squabble for the privilege) against a bald patch in his breast. And when at last he simply must go and eat something in the open leads near by, he just puts the child down on the ice, and twenty chickless Emperors rush to pick it up. And

ABOVE: *Penguins feed their young by going to sea, catching fish or krill, and returning to regurgitate the partly digested prey for the young. This gentoo chick is taking no chances with spillage.*

RIGHT: *All penguins except the emperors and kings lay two eggs, although some raise only one chick to fledging. Here, a gentoo parent is pecked for food by its usual complement of twins.*

they fight over it, and so tear it that sometimes it will die. And, if it can, it will crawl into any ice-crack to escape from so much kindness, and there it will freeze.

The emperors are an extreme case, but for all penguins the struggles of parenthood are considerable. All penguins go to sea to get food for their chicks. When they return some find their chicks easily, in the burrow, where they belong. Some have to thread their way through the big colonies and pick one or two fuzzballs out of a group of fuzzballs. These birds wisely use sound, not sight, to find their young. King penguins returning from the sea may walk right past their chicks and then have to backtrack, using calls to locate each other. To anyone with a scientific mind, this situation calls out (so to speak) for the use of a tape recorder, and such experiments have been done. Scientists played a recording of a chick at the same time as

ABOVE: *The nemesis of penguins in the Antarctic and elsewhere is the skua, a bird that looks a bit like a gull and not only steals penguin eggs but kills and eats the chicks.*

the chick was calling to a returning parent. The parent ignored the loudspeaker. (Obviously, penguins are not stupid.) However, according to Jouventin, "Choice between a chick with a taped bill and a recording of its song... was an insoluble problem, the parents went from one to the other." (Obviously, penguins are not smart, either.) The chicks were also confused. "Several chicks after being successively adopted and abandoned decided to beg to the loudspeaker for adoption!"

A young penguin chasing a parent for food is a sight almost as astonishing as one chasing a tape recorder. I've watched chinstrap and gentoo chicks, almost fully grown, run after a parent, squawking, flapping their wings, sometimes practically climbing up the parent's back. Eventually the adult gives up, stops, turns around, and opens its mouth. The chick fits its beak right inside the adult's. The adult's

ABOVE: *On the Falklands the Johnny rook or caracara, a true bird of prey, takes a toll on the penguin population. Unlike the skua, the Johnny rook is equipped with strong talons and a beak designed to tear flesh.*

stomach then heaves—once, twice, three times—and the partly digested krill spills from the adult's gullet into the chick's. It does so not in a stream, but in soft round balls into which it has been compacted. This method of feeding has produced a peculiar kind of thievery. Small white birds called *sheathbills* try to interrupt feedings and steal what spills on the ground.

At some point, the chicks, like all young everywhere, must go it on their own. In the colonial penguins, the chicks tend to stick together in groups or crèches after they have left the nest but are still being fed by the parents. (Feeding continues until they are fledged and can enter the water.) Together they can fight off the skuas that, at least in the Antarctic, prey on them. In other areas, they may face cats, dogs, stoats, ferrets, giant petrels, true birds of prey (the skuas have neither specialized talons nor a beak for tearing flesh), and other dangers.

The skuas are, however, the most notorious of penguin predators. This may be because they prey only on the young and cute, not the adults. Perhaps it is because they look a bit like big brown sea gulls and don't have the hardware of a true bird of prey, so their kills are neither quick nor clean. Edward Wilson wrote about young Adélie penguins at the Cape Crozier colony:

> They are very funny beasts to watch, and they have a rotten time with the skua gulls which live always near a penguin rookery. For the gulls sit on the young ones' backs, and peck their eyes out and eat them while their mothers are away.

The Brothers Grimm could not have done more for the skua's reputation. The birds are also known for their guile. Sometimes a pair of skuas (they, too, form pair bonds) will work on a penguin sitting on an egg. One attacks from the front and draws the penguin to it, while the other takes the egg. Skuas also know how to work tricks one-on-one. A skua has been known to assault a nesting penguin, drawing it out farther and farther from the nest as it makes defensive sallies. Once the penguin is out far enough, the skua flies over the top of the penguin to the nest behind it, snatches the egg, and flies off.

To kill a chick the skuas must find one alone or isolate it. They seem to do this well. In big penguin colonies in the Antarctic, the skins of dead chicks are everywhere, many with telltale holes in their stomachs, through which the skuas pecked

to get at the innards, and with bald spots on the backs of their heads where the skuas pecked and pecked at an isolated chick until the young penguin was finally felled. One carcass I saw had the bald spot and, in addition, a deformed beak, indicating a bird that would never have made it, skuas or no.

When the penguin colony leaves, of course, the skuas must go back to living on fish and stealing other birds' dinners. (They attack them in the air, making them regurgitate their meal, which the skuas then gobble up.) There is a period, however, when the skuas more or less clean up the few stragglers left. This is when the cardinal sin of penguinhood—asynchrony—acquires a certain poignancy.

Among penguins, it is the young that suffer the "empty-nest" syndrome. The parents, at some point, simply up and leave. In a migratory species like the Adélie,

---

ABOVE: *Two skuas on the Falklands struggle to pull apart a dead baby penguin. Like the penguins on which they prey, skuas share the incubating and raising of their chicks. They often work in pairs to steal eggs or separate a penguin chick from its fellows.*

the adults all go together, and the chicks follow as soon as they can, en masse. They lose their fuzzy down and gain swimming feathers. They walk about flapping their flippers vigorously, apparently getting used to swimming motions, and exercising the appropriate muscles. And eventually, all together, the way Adélies do every-thing (it helps to confuse the leopard seals waiting in the sea for them), the young enter the water.

But not everything works on schedule, not for everyone. I visited King George Island, off the Antarctic Peninsula, where a colony of Adélies is being studied by researchers from the Point Reyes Bird Observatory. This was in February, and most of the Adélies were gone. One Adélie chick was all on its own.

I stood with a group of tourists and watched the chick, still fluffy, being pursued by a skua over the rocky top of a hillside on which all the contours were smoothed and softened by guano. It pecked at the skua and waddled as fast as it could until the skua flew up and dropped down in front of it again. It waddled this way and that, and finally, in desperation, ran over to the tourists. Standing near us, the chick was protected by our presence. The skua was not going to challenge half a dozen well-fed human beings in garish red parkas carrying cameras and video equipment.

This was a classic example (if one can forget the red parkas) of the workings of nature. The skua had to eat; it too had chicks. And who is to say that a skua is worth less than an Adélie penguin? I only wish I could say that I *felt* the truth of this sentiment in the same way that I understand its logic. But that was not my experience. We were told by our guide that the chick had no chance of survival. It would take at least a week for the young penguin to molt into adult plumage, a week without food or a cohort of other chicks, fighting the skua on its own. And there was nothing we could do for it; tourists are not even supposed to touch ani-mals in the Antarctic; and even if some sentimentalist were to have snatched the chick up, what would he have done with it? For the moment, watching the penguin watch us, and the skua watch the penguin, I lost all objectivity and all interest in

---

RIGHT: *The chicks, clockwise from the top left, are: a young king penguin, looking warm and sleepy; a rock hopper almost finished molting from baby down to its adult coat; a molting gentoo; and an Adélie.*

both nature and science. I felt ill. I thought, now I understand why people build cities. I thought, nature is not wonderful, it is abhorrent. I thought of my daughters, six and four. I thought, this is no tour for parents of young children to take.

But finally, with the rest of the tourists, I left the penguin to its skua and the skua to its penguin and walked to an inflatable boat beached on the island's shore, which took us to the tour ship. Once aboard, I sat down in an elegant dining room and had my own very expensive, very good meal, which I ate ravenously, with, I must confess, very little pity for the food. And yet, I am no more a vegetarian than a skua, or for that matter, a penguin is.

ABOVE: *King penguin chicks, feathers wet from rain, look like they are wearing long, ragged fur coats, rather than down. Amid the noisy trumpeting of adults in a colony one can often hear the high peeping of king penguin chicks.*
RIGHT: *Above, a rock hopper adult and chick, both somewhat bedraggled. Below, two rock hoppers quarreling, a common pursuit among penguins.*

4 If Fish Had Wings

ONE CANNOT THINK OF PENGUINS APART FROM THE SEA. I IMAGINE THAT THEY MUST REGARD COMING TO THE ISLAND NOT SO MUCH AS A HOLIDAY, TO BE ENJOYED, AS IN THE LIGHT OF A PAINFUL NECESSITY, TO BE ENDURED.
— Cherry Kearton,
The Island of Penguins, 1930

There is a tradition that the souls of dead sailors inhabit two kinds of seabirds: albatrosses and penguins. The albatross masters the sea by flying over it. The penguin masters the sea by flying in it. Like the penguin, the albatross comes to land only to mate and nest. It does not walk with grace. It does not always take to the air easily. Once in the air, however, it reveals what sort of bird it is. Robert Cushman Murphy compared first seeing an albatross at sea to first seeing a giant Sequoia:

> Much that is well heralded in nature carries a tinge of disappointment when it is finally found. A few things, on the other hand, seem beyond over-advertisement....With a handful of such experiences, in which reality can hardly fail to transcend hope, I would group the sighting of a great albatross at sea.

The birds are indeed inspiring. With a wingspan of eleven feet, a wandering albatross is the biggest, if not the heaviest of flying birds, and the spectacle of it gliding on ocean winds suggests a match of creature and environment unparalleled in the exactness of its fit. Murphy wrote, "Lying on the invisible currents of the breeze, the bird appeared merely to follow its pinkish bill at random."

Albatrosses are transformed by taking to the air. Penguins are transformed by taking to the sea. They don't achieve majesty, but they do shed their comic personas and gather ease and grace about them. It is as if they were circus clowns dropping their costumes to reveal the bodies of acrobats and trapeze artists. Indeed, the entire popular image of penguins is built on seeing them literally out of their element. The extreme juxtapositions, the absurdities that comedy demands, the pratfalls and slapstick—all of these come from the water bird making its way on land.

RIGHT: *Rock hoppers entering the water the hard way. One has taken the leap while others are edging forward.*

Indeed, to love penguins, really to love penguins, you have to be a lover of fish, not birds. Or perhaps a better way to put it is that you have to be in love with the medium in which penguins thrive. You have to have a passion for the sea the way lovers of other birds are infatuated with the air. The real territory of penguins is not the Antarctic or South American coast or the windy islands of the Southern Ocean, but the ocean itself. Penguins are not the creatures of barren, impoverished land that they may seem in breeding season, but creatures of rich, cold seas. Their pastures are swarms of krill and shoals of anchovies, Antarctic fish and squid. And they in turn are food for leopard seals, fur seals, sea lions, sharks, on occasion (for the bigger penguins) killer whales, and even, according to one report, the odd octopus.

And the human reaction to seeing them in the ocean is different to seeing them on land or ice, where the silly little man comes to mind. Cherry Kearton, in a chapter in his book called "Riders of the Sea," wrote of the penguin:

> His element is the sea....When you see him floating, he is no longer comical but entirely beautiful, resting on the moving water, with head raised, a little like a duck; then he suddenly decides to swim, down goes his head, out go his flippers, and like a flash he slips through the water, a streak of black just below the surface.

Edward Wilson, the companion of Scott on his Antarctic journeys, in his diary of the Terra Nova expedition (1910–1912), wrote:

> As we came closer in the number of Adélie Penguins in the water became extraordinary. They were leaping in and out like little dolphins all around us in small schools. I was in the crow's nest nearly the whole time, and the water was as though hundreds of rifle bullets were dropping in around us everywhere.

The description is perfect. When you first see penguins porpoising, unless you have a trained eye, or someone else with a trained eye to enlighten you, what you see is what Wilson described—the rippling pattern of broken water.

That is from a distance. Up close they are different, closer to Kearton's evocation. I've watched gentoo penguins swim near shore in clear, shallow water off a

South Georgia beach, and also in the Central Park Zoo in New York City, just behind a glass window. (Zoos are one of the best places to observe how penguins move underwater, for scientists as well as tourists. Witness papers such as "Kinematics of swimming penguins at the Detroit Zoo.") They are not like fish, quite. Fish often rest, neutrally buoyant, *in*, not *on*, the water. Penguins do not rest under the surface of the water; they are in constant, rapid motion, flying. In the zoo you get to see the kinematics of that flight at close range. The feet are nearly motionless, the flippers beat like the wings they are, and water flows easily around the torpedo bodies, while the slick feathers shed bubble streams of trapped air.

We may try to think of penguins as water birds or even as winged, feathered fish. But the imaginative leap required to have any real sense of what it is like to be a penguin is almost impossible to make. What are the pleasures of fresh krill? What is it like to ride out a storm at sea, *in* the sea? What can the sensations be that attend the dramatic transitions these birds make—from standing in crowded noise amid the overpowering odor of guano, to months at sea in an all-but-unbroken ocean?

The aquatic nature of penguins also poses problems for the scientific imagination and the research that feeds it. How to track penguins at sea? How to study them? Or, to begin at the beginning, how to find them?

The Water Bird

There are some things that are known about penguins as marine creatures, but little with certainty, and nothing completely. In terms of their evolution, the creature that is probably the oldest known penguin was only recently reported on by R. Ewan Fordyce and colleagues. The fossils of this bird were found in New Zealand. The creature seems to have lived about 55 million years ago—well after the dinosaurs disappeared (about 65 million years ago) and well before the time of any creature that was even a remote cousin of a human being. Fordyce's bird has not yet been given a name, but it does seem to be a penguin, though with some characteristics reminiscent of an earlier, flying ancestor.

OVERLEAF: *A group of gentoos returns to shore by the easy route, a flat beach. Gentoos tend not to nest on cliffs but rather on more accessible terrain.*

That earlier ancestor is not known. It is still not possible to trace the first origins of penguins. The paleontologist George Gaylord Simpson suggested that the loss of flight and the transition to the water may have occurred as long as 65 million years ago. And it seems that they may have originated in New Zealand. Again, this riddle can't really be solved with the fossils available, but New Zealand does have an abundance of penguin fossils. In fact, remnants of penguins are among the most common fossil bones found on New Zealand. And New Zealand has had a great diversity of penguins from the time they first appear in the fossil record up to now.

Because the origins of the penguins are cloudy, it's hard to say which other birds are their closest relatives. Biochemical tests of certain proteins suggest one of two orders as most closely related to the penguins, either the *Procellariformes* (a group that includes the albatrosses and petrels) or the *Gaviiformes* (loons). The penguins and albatrosses are not only similar in their proteins, they share some behaviors. Part of the courtship ritual of the wandering albatross is something like the penguin's ecstatic display. In its mating dance the albatross at one point throws its wings back, points its bill to the sky, and neighs. I have a tape recording of this call, and when I play it for non-ornithologists, it is invariably mistaken for the sound of a horse. Certainly the symmetry would be aesthetically pleasing if the penguins and albatrosses were indeed close relatives, one group in the air and the other in the sea, dividing between them the bird kingdom of the Southern Ocean.

What is clearer about the origins of penguins is that they evolved from flying birds. One can see in certain modern birds something like the transitional stage penguins must have gone through, moving from flight in the air to flight in the water. The diving petrels, for instance, are birds that nest in burrows and fly with some difficulty to the ocean, where they feed as they propel themselves underwater with their wings. Penguins passed this stage at some point in their evolution, leaving behind the air for the water. They continue to fly in the new medium, and as their skeletons make clear they retain the keel bone (a sternum or breastbone shaped like a keel), to which the powerful muscles needed for flight are anchored in airborne birds. In the penguin, these powerful muscles are used in similar fashion, to move their wings in a flapping motion—pushing against the liquid medium of the sea as the wings of flyers push against the air.

Naturally, the penguins have evolved wings more suited to water than air. Air is thin and light; it requires a broad, light wing. Water, by comparison, is thick and heavy. It requires a paddle. As Watson puts it in his blunt, descriptive prose, "Their wings are reduced to short, hard flippers covered with scalelike feathers." Having visited penguins in their nesting grounds, and having felt and heard the rush of skuas diving at my head as they flew past, I have naturally wondered what the penguins must feel as they sense the same rush of air. And if penguins can be said to be flying under water, it makes me wonder further whether the krill, squid, and small fish that penguins eat can feel or hear the swift dive of a penguin above them in the same way that a penguin hears the rush of a skua's wings.

The classic penguin shape, described as *fusiform* or *spindle shaped*, is also ideal for the water. It limits drag. Some studies have been done on penguin shape involving mathematical calculations of arcane quantities like the coefficient of drag. What the calculations show, unsurprisingly, is that the penguin's shape is very streamlined. The emperor, in particular, has a shape that is near hydrodynamic perfection.

As to the matter of swimming speeds, here there has been quite a bit of misunderstanding. Early observers thought penguins were swimming "incredibly fast," as Murphy put it. In the past, scientists and others have estimated top speeds at up to 58 kilometers per hour. Actual, documented, measured speeds of penguins show them cruising underwater at average speeds in the 2½-to-7-kilometer-per-hour range. This is very fast walking or easy jogging speed. They seem to be going faster, but perhaps that is merely a suggestion of smooth progress, the aesthetic result on the viewer of a low coefficient of drag. The birds can, of course, swim faster, in short bursts, but maximum speeds are very hard to determine. An emperor, for instance, might well do 15 kilometers per hour for a short distance, or it might do more. Scientists prefer not to guess.

When swimming fast underwater, most penguins "porpoise" to breathe. The reason for this behavior seems to be that the drag at the surface of the water is much

---

OVERLEAF: *Rock hoppers head for the surf en masse, jumping, diving, and falling into the water where it smashes against the rocks. Getting in is the easy part. It is getting back out of the water that is difficult.*

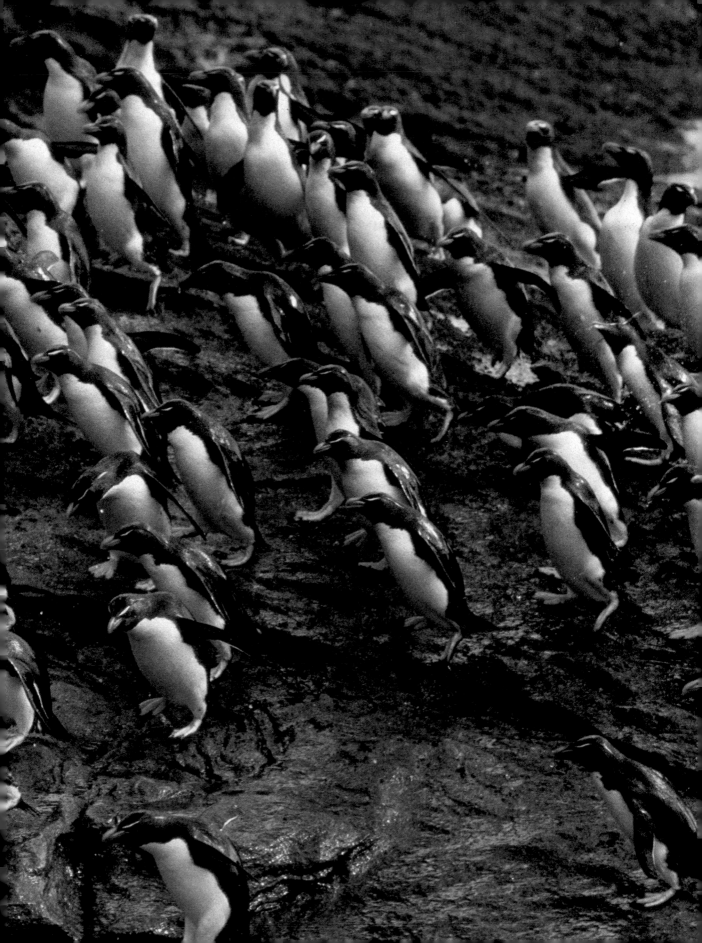

greater than the drag underwater. The most efficient way to get a breath, then, is to leap out of the water, gasp air, and dive back in, rather than surfacing and swimming at the surface while catching a breath. You can hear porpoising penguins gasp for air if you are close enough. As to whether penguins may ever swim fast and leap for the pure irrational, inefficient joy of being in the sea, instead of standing with thousands of other birds in guano, this remains an open question.

The feathering of penguins and the layer of fat the feathers overlay are also designed for the water. Penguins have feathers that trap air in the soft down at their base, and by overlapping the harder, waterproof ends, form a seal to keep the

---

PRECEDING OVERLEAF: *Macaroni penguins in the water and on their way into the water. Like the rock hoppers, macaronis favor cliffs and take their chances with white water when the time comes to go to sea.*

ABOVE: *A Humboldt or Peruvian penguin swimming. Penguins do not use their feet to propel them. They swim with their wings, or flippers, flapping them to propel themselves along. In a sense, they fly underwater.*

air in and the down dry. Penguin feathers are shorter than those of other birds and are packed together more tightly, giving the appearance of fur or scales. I once watched king penguins land in big swells on a South Georgia beach. They were wet, and there was a drizzling rain and a hard wind. The wind whipped the water off their feather coats in beads. Water rolled off them the way a stream from a hose fragments and rolls off the glossy coat of paint on a new car, or the way mercury from a broken thermometer rolls on the floor. Small, spherical droplets raced off their silver backs and deep-black heads.

Penguins are well enough insulated that heat is much more of a problem for most of them than cold. It is a common sight to see penguins standing in the sun (there is no shade) on the Antarctic peninsula with flippers out, the undersides flushed pink. The color comes from blood circulating near the surface, helping the birds shed heat. On hot summer days, which for birds like Adélies in the Antarctic could be in the 40°F range, the penguins gravitate to any ice or snow they can find.

Because penguin insulation comes mostly from trapped air and not from blubber, penguins can't afford to have a leak in their waterproof shield of feathers—and yet feathers wear out. All birds molt, replacing their feathers. Some do it a bit at a time, all year long. The penguins do it all at once, on land or ice, usually some time after breeding. They will go to sea to fatten up once again and then come ashore or board an ice floe to molt. Molting makes great demands on their stored energy. Adélies lose up to 50 percent of their body weight during a three-week molt. While they are molting, they cannot enter the water to eat.

One of the other demands on a seagoing, air-breathing creature that dives for its food is that it has to be able to hold its breath and deal with the greater pressures of deep water. Gerald L. Kooyman of the Scripps Institute of Oceanography in La Jolla, California, is the leading authority on penguin adaptations to diving, and he has found that in general most of the penguins make fairly short and shallow dives, a minute or two, with maximum depths of 70 or 100 meters and those not common.

OVERLEAF: *Penguins swimming fast, like these macaronis, move along underwater and then leap out to take a breath. Without the camera to stop the action, porpoising penguins move so fast they could be mistaken for fish breaking water.*

The emperors and the kings are much deeper divers. The deepest recorded dives of emperor penguins, which are also the deepest known dives of any bird, are to depths of more than 350 meters, well over 1,000 feet, and the longest dive ever recorded was eighteen minutes. Both figures are unusual; their dives are more commonly in the four-minute range, not that much longer than those of other, smaller penguins. But both the emperors and kings do make deeper dives than other penguins, perhaps because their main prey of fish may be found deeper than the krill and other crustaceans and fish that most penguins eat.

The diving abilities of penguins are not that well understood. Those of marine mammals like the Weddell seal have been more thoroughly studied. (This seal has some of the deepest known dives—to 1,970 feet—of marine mammals, except for whales.) The blood of Weddell seals has a greater oxygen-carrying capacity than that of human beings, for instance, and its muscles have higher concentrations of myoglobin, which binds and stores oxygen. It also has reinforced airways, and when it dives, it expels breath from its lungs. In the course of the dive it is not taking nitrogen at high pressure from the lungs into its bloodstream. Consequently, this nitrogen is not going to fizz out of the blood when, on the seal's ascent, the pressure decreases, and the seal is not going to succumb to nitrogen narcosis, or the bends.

The oxygen-carrying capacity of penguins' blood is greater than that of some other birds, according to Kooyman, but not really exceptional. Their heart rate may go down during diving, resulting in a decreased need for oxygen, but that isn't for certain. They do have quite a high concentration of myoglobin in their muscles, as do other diving birds and mammals. As to the bends, the smaller penguins, with their shallower and shorter dives, may not face the problem of nitrogen narcosis at all. But that would not hold for the emperors and kings. Moreover, they are not constructed the way the Weddell seal is. Penguins, like other birds, store more air in air sacs connected to the lungs than in the lungs themselves. When they dive, they do not expel breath, and during a dive they do take up oxygen into their blood-

PRECEDING OVERLEAF: *When penguins are swimming slowly, or resting, like these gentoos, they hold their heads above water, paddling along with their flippers, looking something like geese, or loons.*

stream from the air sacs, where, presumably, air, including nitrogen, is under high pressure. What happens to the nitrogen, and why the birds don't suffer on some of the deeper, longer dives, is an unknown.

At Sea

Almost all of the studies of penguins in the water, as Kooyman likes to point out, have been done on birds making relatively short feeding forays from breeding grounds on land. He has written of penguins, "The great majority of their time is spent at sea yet the vast majority of information on their life history is on birds ashore." The reason for this is that the oceans in which penguins swim are vast and remote. The shores and islands on which they breed are less so. The birds are concentrated in the breeding colonies, and the difficulty of finding and following them is enormously reduced. Scientists who study penguins and are striving to understand them have to proceed a bit like the proverbial drunk looking for his lost keys under a streetlight. The keys are more likely to be out in the darkness somewhere, but the streetlight is the only place he can see to look.

By looking under their own particular streetlight, scientists who study penguins have, for instance, learned quite a bit about their eating habits. All penguins eat some kind of fish or crustaceans or other marine creatures. But the diets vary from species to species. The deep-diving emperors and kings eat fish and squid mostly. The little blue penguin is a fish eater, as is the yellow-eyed penguin. The crested penguins eat a varied diet, some relying more heavily on fish and squid, and others, like the macaroni, being more dependent on krill. The three small Antarctic penguins all depend primarily on krill, at least in the Antarctic, although the gentoo eats more fish.

All the *Spheniscus* penguins are fish eaters, usually small fish like anchovies that are found in large shoals. And these penguins can be found in large groups themselves, sometimes up to 200, with other seabirds, feeding on the fish when they are abundant. They have sharp bills, constructed with a hook at the end of the upper bill and a cleft at the end of the lower bill. The bills fit together in such a way as to prevent a fish that the bird has snapped up from getting loose. All the penguins have on their tongues and palates a backwards-facing carpet of stiff, fleshy bristles which, John Warham of New Zealand writes, "presumably assist in the handling of still-moving prey and in directing food back down the gullet." I think the notion of food that needs to be directed *back* down the gullet captures in one image the nature of penguin cuisine.

To understand further how and where the birds go about feeding, some studies with radio tracking have been done of penguins at their breeding colonies. Wayne and Susan Trivelpiece of the Point Reyes Bird Observatory in California have been doing a variety of studies of the three brush-tailed penguins—chinstraps, gentoos, and Adélies—on King George Island near the Antarctic Peninsula. In one study they and their coworkers glued thumb-sized transmitters with a wire antenna between the shoulder blades of about half a dozen gentoo penguins and about the same number of chinstrap penguins. Then, using two tracking stations, they followed the birds as they went about their foraging trips in Admiralty Bay. The gentoos dived for about two minutes on average, and the chinstraps for about ninety seconds, the same as Adélies, judging from other studies. Gentoos also return to feed their chicks more frequently—every twelve or so hours—as compared to the chinstraps, which average trips of sixteen or seventeen hours, and the Adélies, which stay out foraging for twenty-four hours. The Trivelpiece's conclusion is that the gentoos are able to dive deeper and find more food closer to shore. This would make sense since gentoos are bigger birds, and size is very closely correlated with diving ability in birds.

A colleague of the Trivelpieces at the Point Reyes Bird Observatory, David Ainley, has worked with another scientist there, Bill Fraser, to do some of the few studies of penguins during the Austral winter, following Adélies and chinstraps in the Weddell Sea. Chinstraps had been thought to share the pack ice with Adélies in the winter, when the pancake-flat floes of sea ice, interrupted by small stretches of open water, extend hundreds of miles out from the Antarctic Continent into the surrounding ocean. Fraser and Ainley found that this was not true. The Adélies were indeed congregating on ice floes and bits of bergs, feeding in the open water near them, but the chinstraps were not. Chinstraps were observed in open water, in the ocean beyond the pack-ice belt. Furthermore, Fraser and Ainley put together

---

RIGHT: *Emperor penguins "fly" beneath the Antarctic ice, looking for the squid they feed on. Emperors are the deepest-diving penguins. The longest dive recorded for an emperor was 18 minutes, and the deepest went to more than 800 feet.*

their observations with the studies of the Trivelpiece's and found that Adélies and chinstraps mirrored each other in their winter survival rates. One year Adélie populations would be up 15 percent and chinstraps down roughly the same amount. Another year the situation would be reversed. The changes were connected to the amount of pack ice. In years when the pack-ice belt extended farther out from the continent than in more mild winters, the Adélies did well and the chinstraps poorly. In milder years, with less pack ice, the chinstraps did well and the Adélies poorly.

We also know a bit about what some other penguins do. The magellanic penguins have a pelagic (or seagoing) phase in which, on the west coast of South America, they venture as far north as Brazil, and 150 kilometers out to sea. The emperors do not migrate to the open sea but stay in the regions of ice year round. And the king penguins, with their staggered breeding cycles, may go to sea for weeks at a time,

ABOVE: *A Galápagos penguin in the waters near its home. The Galápagos penguins, like most of the other banded penguins, are fish eaters.*

but not for several months. Still, no one has tracked these birds at sea and charted their behavior and activity. The yellow-eyed penguins, little penguins, and Galápagos penguins are all nonmigratory, going to sea only for short feeding trips. The gentoos stick near home.

Such studies are small glimmers of brightness in the large area of obscurity and darkness outside the streetlight, away from the breeding colonies. And it will be some time before we learn more. Research is beginning now on sea mammals, for instance, with transmitters that can be tracked by satellite. But these are still too big for any but the biggest penguins to wear without interference; they weigh about twenty-five grams and are the size of a cigarette pack. Sooner or later transmitters will be developed that are powerful enough, small enough, and cheap enough to put on penguins. The size is important because, as Gerald Kooyman points out, penguins and sea mammals are "so clean, hydrodynamically" that anything attached to them disturbs their lines. What must be achieved to acquire good information is a transmitter that, over a long period of time, is not going to bother the penguin enough to change or impair its behavior.

Among the real mysteries that remain is the off-season life of the crested penguins. They all go to sea from between four to six months after they are finished with breeding and molting. The rock hoppers and macaronis are gone for a full six months and head for the open sea. What they do there, how they groom themselves, what social groupings they have, their feeding behavior during that time—all these questions are open.

In thinking about the nature of penguins it is these times that draw the imagination. The notion of millions of birds surviving for months at sea in unknown regions is profoundly more exciting than those same millions on land. It is because of the seagoing life of a penguin that a sailor would want his reincarnated soul to inhabit the bird. It is in these oceanic travels that the birds have their kinship with their cousins the wandering albatrosses. It has to be there, at sea, that penguins feel most at home.

OVERLEAF: *The little blue penguin, from Australia, is the smallest of all penguins. It feeds primarily on fish, while the larger chinstraps, Adélies, and gentoos of the Antarctic subsist largely on the shrimplike krill.*

5 Close Encounters

THE ENTRIES IN MY DIARY AT THIS TIME ARE ALL IN TELE-GRAPHIC STYLE, NO DOUBT OWING TO THE AMOUNT OF WORK. THUS AN ENTRY IN FEBRUARY ENDS WITH THE FOLLOWING WORDS: "AN EMPEROR PENGUIN JUST COME ON A VISIT—SOUP-KETTLE."
—Roald Amundsen, *The South Pole*

Penguins live, and have lived, on the periphery of human consciousness, much as they live on the periphery of continents and islands. Their oldest associations with us have been on the coasts of New Zealand, Australia, South Africa, and South America. More recently they have shared the seas with explorers, sealers, whalers, scientists, and tourists. It may be that human beings always thought penguins were cute, but there is no evidence that this is so. Until very recent times, by far the most common interaction between the two species, when we have met, has been one in which *we* ate *them*.

In Tierra del Fuego, at the tip of South America, the Indians killed penguins for their meat and skins. The penguin population at large was never threatened; there were many, many penguins, and—even in their heyday—not so many Fuegians. Other South American Indians also used penguin meat and skins. In the times before Europeans explored and colonized these places, the Maoris of New Zealand and the natives of South Africa may have eaten penguins or their eggs, but we don't know for sure.

Europeans continued the tradition. They first encountered penguins during a period of heroic maritime exploration of the globe and accompanying privation on the part of the heroic maritime explorers. A primary ingredient in this privation was hunger, and penguins—fat, plentiful, unafraid, and less than swift on land—were a welcome solution. The very first penguins seen may not have been killed and eaten, but if not, they were the only ones.

It seems that the first Europeans to see penguins were also the first Europeans to round the southern tip of Africa in 1487–88 with Bartolomeu Dias de Novaes.

RIGHT: *King penguins on South Georgia Island, overshadowed by a cruise ship. More and more tourists are going to the Antarctic and other wild destinations to see penguins.*

Dias probably saw penguins, but he left no record of observing them. Vasco da Gama later followed Dias's example and route in 1497. A record of this voyage does exist and seems to mention penguins, but it was not published until 1838. This report, quoted by George Gaylord Simpson, gave the bird a confusing name of uncertain source and meaning, but the other details leave little doubt about just what creature was being described:

> On the same island there are birds as big as ducks, but they cannot fly, because they have no feathers on their wings. These birds, of whom we killed as many as we chose, are called Fotylicavos, and they bray like asses.

The first published account of penguins came out of Magellan's voyage. Magellan, who was killed in the Philippines, only partway through the first circumnavigation of the globe, had along with him a passenger who is sometimes described as the first round-the-world tourist. This was Antonio Pigafetta, an Italian noblemen who booked passage on Magellan's voyage simply to be part of it. Pigafetta kept a journal, which was published, and he did mention penguins, but before I get to that, I would like to argue that it would be more appropriate to call him an adventurer, since he willingly entered into an expedition that offered every opportunity for a miserable death. It is hard to grasp how routine it was for men on these exploratory voyages to suffer and die. They fell in battle, were executed for mutiny, and rotted away of disease and starvation.

Oddly enough, one of the most graphic accounts of such misery and desperation involves penguins themselves. It is the sort of story that Poe would have been happy to have invented, but it comes from an old chronicle of the exploration of the Americas, *The Last Voyage of the Worshipful M. Thomas Candish, Esquire*, written by one John Jane. The particular part of the voyage relating to penguins begins when an island full of the birds is discovered in the Strait of Magellan:

> When wee were come to this Isle wee sent out boate on shore, which returned laden with birdes and egges; and our men sayd that the Penguins were so thicke upon the Isle, that shippes might be laden with them; for they could not goe without treading upon the birds, whereat we greatly rejoiced.

The sailors killed the penguins and dried them. They did not salt the birds down, as was often done with penguins, and from my reading of the story, that was their big mistake. What happened on the return voyage as the ship approached the Equator with its penguin cargo cannot be summarized. It can only be quoted:

> But after we came neere unto the sun, our dried Penguins began to corrupt, and there bred in the[m] a most lothsome and ugly worme of an inch long. This worme did so mightily increase and devoure our victuals, that there was in reason no hope how we should avoide famine, but be devoured of these wicked creatures: there was nothing that they did not devoure, only yron excepted: our clothes, boots, shooes, hats, shirts, stockings: and, for the ship, they did so eat the timbers as that we greatly feared they would undoe us by gnawing through the ships side. Great was the care and diligence of our captaine, master, and company to consume these vermine, but the more we laboured to kill them the more they increased; so that at the last we could not sleepe for them, for they would eate our flesh and bite like Mosquitos.

Eventually, the crew fell ill of some awful disease, perhaps related to malnutrition but not explicitly connected to the penguins and their worms. "And some died in most lothsome and furious paine." Of seventy-six men, only sixteen were alive when the ship landed at Bear-haven in Ireland on June 11, in 1593. Magellan's men did not fare much better. Pigafetta survived, although he was wounded in the Philippines as he was fighting alongside Magellan in the battle in which the captain was killed (as I said, "tourist" is too deprecatory a term for this sort of traveling). But nine-tenths of those who set out on the trip did not make it home. Had I been on one of these voyages I too would have rejoiced at the sight of fat penguins, and eaten them without qualm.

Pigafetta's journal was circulated privately at first and later was published in Paris in a French translation in or about 1525. It may have provided Shakespeare with the name of the Patagonian devil Setebos, which he used in *The Tempest*. It certainly provided the world with the first published account of penguins, which Pigafetta called *strange geese*.

After following the coast towards the Antarctic pole, they came to two
islands full of geese and sea wolves in such numbers that in one hour they
were able to fill their five ships with geese, and they are completely black
and unable to fly and they live on fish, and are so fat that it is necessary to
peel them; they do not have feathers and have a beak like a crow.

Simpson notes that he finds it odd that Pigafetta called the birds *geese*, since
penguins don't resemble them. Here, despite his historical and scientific thoroughness and accuracy, I think Simpson missed the boat, or perhaps the bird. To someone who hasn't devoted himself to either birds or taxonomy, there is a great deal of
common ground between penguins and geese. Both are large. Both float in the
water (sometimes) with their heads up. True, penguins look more like loons or cormorants when in this posture, but, and this is the real point, Pigafetta's acquain-
tance with birds, of any sort, may have been concentrated largely on those he
encountered at table. My guess is that the comparison is a case of form or rather
perceived form, following function, or rather, use. Geese were large, fat, and edible.
So were penguins.

Whatever the reason, from Vasco da Gama's voyage onward, the early accounts
of penguins frequently have to do with the harvesting of the birds. And the goose
comparison surfaces often. John Jane knew the birds by name but chose a similar
comparison to Pigafetta's:

This Penguin hath the shape of a bird, but hath no wings, only two stumps in
the place of wings, by which he swimmeth under water with as great swiftnes
as any fish. They live upon smelts, whereof there is great abundance upon
this coast: in eating they be neither fish nor flesh: they lay great eggs, and
the bird is of a reasonable bignes, very near twise so big as a ducke.

Penguin Cuisine

Eventually, of course, the duck and goose were replaced by the little man in dinner
dress. But, whatever the reaction of explorers to penguins, whether they were
singing songs to the birds, dancing with them on ice floes, laughing at their antics,

or clubbing them aside due to annoyance or scientific interest, they continued to dine on them. Recipes and opinions on the quality of penguin cuisine varied.

Thaddeus von Bellingshausen, writing about his 1819 voyage in Antarctic waters:

> We had [penguin] stewed together with salt beef and gruel and seasoned with vinegar; the crew liked it seeing that the officers' mess too pronounced favourably upon it.

James Clark Ross, in a diary entry for 1841, made during his Antarctic explorations:

> We saw several of the large penguins, and three were brought on board: they were very powerful birds, and we had some difficulty in killing them …their flesh is very dark, and of a rank fishy flavour.

ABOVE: *Remote locations are no longer a guarantee of freedom from human activity. Here a gentoo penguin on a Falkland Islands beach lies caught in fragments of a fishing net.*

The indefatigable Edward Wilson, off New Zealand:

> The penguin's flesh is black but has nothing unpleasant about it at all, so long as the fat is avoided, which is very much like cod liver oil. I could live comfortably on the meat, and the eggs are most delicious, neither rank nor different in any way from fowls' eggs and very pale.

On Adélies in the Ross Sea:

> Stewed, they were delicious, but fried in butter in "blessed mouthfuls" they were heavenly.

Or, on his last voyage, of the other truly Antarctic species:

> Spent forenoon skinning the Emperor—a male, very fat. Half the breast and the liver was a substantial meal for 16 men with nothing else but some peas, cocoa, and biscuit. We fried it in butter and it was excellent.

Otto Nordenskjöld's 1901 expedition, which overwintered on an island off the east and colder coast of the Antarctic Peninsula, depended greatly on penguins, and he wrote that he loathed killing them. A week's menu for his party included the following penguin dishes: "breast of penguin and dried vegetables ... salted penguin and beans ... salted penguin ... penguin and macaroni or rice ... pastry and cold penguin ... sardines and cold penguin."

The eggs of penguins were also relished by seafarers and others. The American sealer Edmund Fanning wrote of his voyages to the Falklands in the early nineteenth century, "The eggs most preferred of all that the South Sea country produces, are those of the Mackaronie penguin."

In the Falkland Islands, egging, or gathering penguin eggs, is a tradition. For many years November 9 was a holiday devoted to collecting penguin eggs. On

---

RIGHT: *When tourists visit the king penguins on South Georgia Island, their presence sometimes causes a ripple effect. As they edge nearer the colony, the penguins on the periphery move inward, crowding their neighbors and setting off a wave of shuffling, trumpeting, and pecking.*

another continent, the eggs of jackass penguins used to be sold in the markets of Capetown, South Africa. In fact, although all the other culinary depredations put together have probably not made a serious dent in penguin populations, the collection of eggs may have been a major cause of the decline of the jackass penguin on the islands off South Africa. Legal egging ceased in 1968, but in its heyday, in the 1920s, half a million eggs were taken each year off Dassen Island (the Penguin Island of Cherry Kearton's book). By some estimates there are now about 200,000 black-footed penguins left, about 5 percent of the population that once existed.

Penguin Oil, and Oiled Penguins

Penguins have had other encounters with human beings. They have been killed and rendered for their oil, as were elephant seals, and, of course, whales. The lesser creatures were usually used to supplement the oil gathered in whaling voyages. However, starting in 1891 one New Zealander ran a business for twenty-five years on Macquarie Island boiling down kings and royal penguins for their oil. Public outcry finally forced the government to cancel the concession they had granted him. The man, Joseph Hatch, claimed that the royal penguins were more numerous at the end of his tenure than when he started. Simpson writes, "In fact he was probably right. He was taking only a small fraction of the population, and the remaining breeding pairs were quite capable of at least of replacing the loss." That small fraction was 150,000 birds a year.

Penguins have also suffered from the mining of guano on the islands off South America. Tons and tons of guano were mined on the islands off Peru, where it sometimes existed in deposits 180 feet deep. Penguins and other seabirds burrowed into this old, dried guano to make their nests. And now the Peruvian or Humboldt penguin, common in zoos, is in trouble. There are few estimates of its population along the coast of northern Chile and Peru and offshore. But it was once abundant, and it is no longer.

As seabirds, penguins naturally face yet another hazard, the legacy of an oil-based human economy to marine birds and mammals—the oil spill. The route around the Cape of Good Hope is a major one for supertankers. One spill in 1968 of 4,000 tons of oil is estimated to have killed about 15,000 of the already hard-hit black-footed penguins. The magellanic penguins of Argentina also suffer from oil in the water, which results from oil tankers cleaning out their tanks. According to Dee Boersma, about 10 percent of banded Punta Tombo birds found dead each year have perished because of the oil. And these are not chicks. They are juveniles and breeding adults, with years of reproduction ahead of them, during which they help to maintain the colony.

Penguin Science

Penguins also encounter human beings through the lens of science. From our side this lens provides a vast amount of information that helps us learn how the world works—information that may well keep us from destroying Antarctica, its ocean, and its penguins. In achieving this end, the depredations of science have been both rare and small, and for a good end. But this has doubtless not always been apparent to the individual penguins involved, looking at the events, as they did, through the other end of the lens. Early natural-history studies were based on the killing of birds, or the "collecting of specimens," as it is sometimes called. Charles Wilkes, who was in charge of the United States Exploring Expedition to the Antarctic (1838–42), gave an account of this early scientific pursuit. In this case he was on Macquarie Island, on his way to the Antarctic, in a rock hopper colony:

> As we wanted a number of specimens, I commenced kicking them down the precipice, and knocked on the head those which had the temerity to attack me …

Later he changed his mind:

> It was now time to return to the boat, when it occurred to me that live birds would be preferable to the dead; so throwing the latter down, I seized one old and a couple of young ones, and with three or four eggs in my cap, made the best of my way to the boat.

I don't mean to suggest, however, that penguins suffered in the collecting any more than any other creature. Audubon shot countless birds for his paintings. The American Museum of Natural History is full of slain elephants, gorillas, and gnus. That was the way the discipline of natural history was pursued.

"DISCOVERY"

THE

SOUTH POLAR TIMES.

APRIL · 1902

Title page of first issue of *South Polar Times*, April 1902

Today, penguins are protected in most areas. And field science more often demands inconvenience instead of the ultimate sacrifice from its subjects. To establish breath-holding abilities, birds have sometimes been "dived"—in other words, forced under water. The penguins don't seem to like it. When researchers study the feeding habits of penguins they must catch them, put a tube down their gullets, pour salt water down the tube, and then hold the birds upside down so that they will regurgitate the food they have just caught. It's worth remembering, however, that penguins in general may benefit from these studies. Findings of this sort of research help us develop a picture of the Antarctic ecosystem (who dives where to eat what) so that we will know the consequences of intervention, such as harvesting krill, which some nations are experimenting with.

Sometimes modern scientific enterprises exact a heavier toll. The building of an airstrip at a French research base on Antarctica in Adélie Land caused quite a stir between Greenpeace environmental activists and the French. Greenpeace charged that the building of the strip had killed a thousand penguins, and activists who had traveled by ship from Australia to the research station ended up in physical fights with construction workers.

Still, none of this is peculiar to penguins. As far as suffering from human enterprise goes, penguins have done all right, compared to whales or passenger pigeons. Most penguins are holding their own these days. The Peruvian or Humboldt penguin and the black-footed penguin are in difficulty, as is the yellow-eyed penguin. The Galápagos penguin numbers probably no more than 6,000 birds, although that may have little to do with human activity. In Chile, the magellanic penguins are sometimes used for bait to catch king crabs. There is movement to stop this use of them, but there are still many, many magellanic penguins. As a species they are not in danger.

The Antarctic penguins are thriving. Some, like the chinstraps, are increasing in numbers. It may be that here, human beings have actually aided the penguins. We have come close to eliminating some of the big whales that feed on krill in the Southern Ocean. The penguins also feed on krill, and they have a lot more to eat

LEFT: *The first issue of the* South Polar Times, *a newspaper put out during Robert Scott's Antarctic expedition on the* Discovery, *memorialized the emperor penguin.*

than they did in the early years of this century when modern factory whaling in the far southern seas began.

Zoos

This is not the whole history of human beings and penguins, of course. There are the separate discoveries of each species. There are quite touching and silly descriptions of sailors' interactions with penguins. And disgraceful stories of mistreatment for no other reason than carelessness or insensitivity. And there is also the history of collection for zoos.

At first this was a grim business, since many of the penguins collected died in transition to their new homes. On boats, or even airplanes, heat killed them. And when they got to their new locations, avian malaria, the fungus disease aspergillosis, and bacterial infections laid them low. In 1958, to take one example, thirty-seven penguins were flown into a new zoo in Portland, Oregon. Within weeks six emperors and five Adélies were dead of aspergillosis. In 1965 a press release from the National Science Foundation described the collecting of fifty-four Adélie penguins, "ten couples, twenty-eight babies and six single adults" from the Antarctic. But, "unknown to the penguins and seals, the aircraft developed engine trouble at Nandi in the Fiji Islands and had to return to Christchurch. Four of the birds died from overheating."

Because the true Antarctic penguins pose enormous difficulties for zoos, the more common birds on exhibit are black-footed penguins and Peruvian penguins, from temperate regions. They live outdoors and are actually, in contrast to what most zoo visitors think, quite comfortable in the summer. In fact, the cold weather is a problem for them. A black-footed penguin at the New York Aquarium on Coney Island lost its toes to frostbite one cold winter day.

Among the zoos that have been successful at penguin keeping, the Edinburgh Zoo has one of the longest records. But Sea World in San Diego has the largest and most elaborate facility in the world, the Penguin Encounter, a huge refrigerated exhibit designed for research and for public viewing. In fact the Sea World facility had the honor of making the professional journal *Air Conditioning & Refrigeration News* when it was completed in 1983. And no wonder. The Encounter is a

28,000-square-foot refrigerator, or perhaps freezer is a better word. The air temperature is kept at 28°F. The saltwater pool stays at 45°F and there is equipment to produce 12,000 pounds of fresh ice each day for the penguins to stand and walk around on, to eat, and to use in preening themselves.

The exhibit houses about 400 birds from seven different species: emperor, Adélie, king, macaroni, chinstrap, gentoo, and rock hopper. Visitors stand on a moving walkway as it goes past a 100-foot-long viewing window looking in at an area of 3,000 square feet (the rest is not on public view) with penguins, kelp gulls, and the notoriously uncute blue-eyed shags as well. There is an outdoor exhibit area for magellanic penguins, and a separate breeding area for Humboldt penguins.

The lighting system for the Antarctic birds mimics the Austral cycle—dark in our summer, light in our winter. The facility is designed to allow research and to be self-sustaining. In fact, the first emperor penguin ever to hatch outside the Antarctic did so at Sea World in 1980, when the birds were still housed in a private 3,800-square-foot freezer. More than 200 Adélies have been hatched and reared there since 1976. The kings have also reproduced. And among the numerous scientific studies at the Sea World facility, one showed that the sex of emperor penguins can be determined by their trumpeting.

The person largely responsible for the Penguin Encounter—in fact, by accounts of other penguin keepers, for the presence of any Antarctic penguins at all in zoos in the United States—is Frank Todd. No longer with Sea World, Todd has his own consulting company, but working with Sea World and the National Science Foundation, he led the establishment of the Sea World colony over almost two decades in the Antarctic. At first, to fight the problem of overheating, the birds were flown to refrigerated exhibits in refrigerated airplanes. Todd said of one such flight, "I was a hell of a lot colder than I ever was in the Antarctic." When a door was opened during a stopover in Hawaii, it snowed inside the airplane. "The birds thrived; we didn't."

And in 1983 Sea World began collecting penguins by gathering not the birds, but the eggs, and putting them into incubators. In contrast to the adult birds, particularly

OVERLEAF: *A researcher participating in a breeding study of gentoo penguins on South Georgia Island nudges an adult with a long pole to see the eggs it is incubating.*

those from the Antarctic, the eggs do not suffer from the stress of capture and flying. They do not need to be refrigerated. They need to be kept warm, and not broken, but that is more easily achieved. And when the birds are hatched in captivity, there is no stress in adjusting to their new home.

Ease of collection and transportation were not, however, the only reasons this system of egg gathering was developed. The fundamental rationale, according to Todd, was that it was less damaging to penguin populations. Most penguins lay more than one egg, but seldom raise to fledging more than one chick. In collecting from these species, one egg would be taken from a two-egg clutch. Those eggs were destined to be lost, or, as Todd puts it, as far as the natural population of penguins and their destined growth are concerned, "All the birds that were raised from those eggs are birds that don't exist."

Another very new penguin facility is in Central Park Zoo, in the middle of New York City. This facility is also refrigerated and contains chinstrap and gentoo penguins. A glass window fronts on the pool, and visitors can watch the penguins above water, and swimming under water. It is a superb way to see how the animals swim. All of these penguins were collected as eggs, most during a 1986 Sea World expedition. When the New York Zoological Society rebuilt and redesigned the Central Park Zoo, creating the penguin exhibit, it traded tufted puffins to Sea World for the penguins.

These penguins were all hand raised, which can sometimes cause problems. Penguins that have been treated something like children may relate so strongly to their human benefactors that they fail to relate to other penguins. They fixate on the person feeding them as a parent. At the Coney Island Aquarium there is a penguin called Klousseau, after the Peter Sellers' comic character. Klousseau, rejected by his parents and facing starvation, was hand raised with a view to training him. The senior keeper in charge of the penguins, Peter Fenimore, told me that the problem was the training did not go well. "After a couple of years they found out about the only thing he could be trained to do was walk behind you, and they stuck him back in the colony." Now he is aggressive and wants all the attention at feeding time, practically trying to get in the keeper's lap. Presumably Klousseau feels that by some horrible mistake he is a person forced to live with a lot of *birds*.

In contrast, the birds at the Central Park Zoo, benefiting from the example of Klousseau and others like him that had gone before them, always had the company of other penguins as well as people while they were being raised. The result, according to James Murtaugh, the curator of animals at the Central Park Zoo, is that, "These birds, in effect, see both themselves and us as penguins."

For penguins in captivity, disease is a constant problem. In Central Park all the air going into the exhibit is filtered down to a level of three microns. The pool water is constantly filtered and occasionally replaced. The synthetic rocks of the exhibit are covered with a clear acrylic to prevent damage to the birds' feet and the resultant, unhappy condition of bacterial infection, or bumblefoot. The rocks, which accumulate guano faster than a penguin can say Ark!, are wetted down by an automated spraying system twice daily, and once a day a zoo worker uses a pressure sprayer to clean the rocks more carefully.

Even so, penguins do die. In the first year of the exhibit one bird was lost to aspergillosis and another to a pernicious and dangerous ailment that also kills wild animals and may someday strangle all nonautomated entities on the entire planet. Zoo people call it "hardware disease." The bird had eaten a piece of plastic, which perforated its intestine.

The final arena of human and penguin contact is tourism. Penguins aren't easy to get to, but they can be seen. At Punta Tombo in Argentina, where Dee Boersma works, the magellanic penguins are there in the hundreds of thousands. In Australia, one can go to the beach and see the little blue penguins, the smallest of all. Tours to the Galápagos are almost commonplace these days. And then there is the Antarctic itself and the vast cold moat of the Southern Ocean that surrounds it.

Today there are only a few ships that take tourists to Antarctica, to South Georgia, and to the Falklands, but the number grows each year. There are apparently enough people with enough money to support the enormously expensive business of

---

OVERLEAF: *Falkland Island rock hoppers parade past two boys. Until recently, penguin eggs were regularly consumed on the Falklands, and November 9 was a traditional holiday devoted to collecting the eggs.*

tourism in the far South. The experience of being on the Southern Ocean as a tourist is an odd one. You travel on a luxurious passenger liner, with bars, dining rooms, a library, a choice of fine wines. People who work on the cruise ship hold the rubber boats for you as you embark from the ship and disembark on remote islands, often almost lifting you out while they stand waist- or chest-deep (wearing rubber waders and long underwear) in the freezing swells. You look for whales and penguins from the enclosed observation deck, thinking of sailors fighting the weather off Cape Horn, suffering frostbite (one story tells of a sailor who blew on his frostbitten nose—it fell off). And then you land to look at penguins as you are led by guides and accompanied by scores of other tourists all wearing orange parkas.

Even when you are surrounded by other tourists, the impact of a mass of colonial penguins is powerful. The sheer force of nature is inescapable. What conservationists worry about is the other side of the coin: the impact of colonial tourists on the penguins. There are differences of opinion. Well-run tours (as mine was) insist on the least disturbance possible. But there are always people who feel that a picture is worth a thousand penguins. I watched one couple in which the man, holding the video camera that is to an Antarctic tourist as a sun hat is to a tropical one, kept motioning his wife forward toward penguins on a rock outcrop near the sea. He wanted pictures of them diving. He wanted her to herd them into the water. The penguins, though agitated, did not comply. (I should point out that, contrary to everything you might expect, the man was not American, but Swiss.)

William Conway, director of the New York Zoological Society, who has a long involvement with the penguins of Punta Tombo, believes tourism to wild areas can be worthwhile, mostly if it brings income to a local human population, thus providing an economic incentive to protect the creatures that are drawing the tourists. There is, of course, no local population in the Antarctic, and Conway is not overly optimistic about the benefits of Antarctic tourism or the future of Antarctic penguins, even though the birds are now doing well. Any increase in human activity in the Antarctic threatens them, he says, with greater chances for accidents like the oil spill that occurred in 1989 near Palmer Station on Anvers Island, off the Antarctic peninsula. Conway's forecast is grim: He sees human activity increasing inevitably, believes penguin populations should be carefully monitored, and says, "I'm afraid that I think many of them will be lost in the fullness of time."

George Gaylord Simpson, writing in 1976, thought tourism on the whole was beneficial to penguins, since the tourists came because they loved the birds, tended to leave them alone, and left loving them more than they did when they began. Bernard Stonehouse, one of the foremost researchers on penguins, is a supporter of Antarctic tourism if it is pursued with care. At the time of the oil spill that Conway referred to, Stonehouse was in the Antarctic, and he was concerned that the name of tourism not be blackened. He believes that it can create support for preservation of wildlife. In some cases, tourists have even acted as whistle blowers, calling attention to abuses of wildlife they found while traveling.

In all of this what strikes me as most ironic is that it is the least realistic image of the penguin, the one most clouded by our own habits or thought and dress—that of the man in white tie and tails—that has brought the birds to our attention, and that in no small part inspires a desire to protect them. Penguins have a claim on us that snail darters and crocodilians and insects will never have. By an accident of evolution that set them upright and waddling and gave them a severe and attractive color scheme, they remind us of ourselves. They are jesters of a sort. We too squawk and fight, and foul our own cities. But we are not cute. The future of penguins may be far from sure, but they have a better chance than many other creatures. The might even help save an ecosystem or two—all by walking funny and dressing for dinner.

ACKNOWLEDGMENTS

First of all, I am grateful to
the many people I inter-
viewed for the time they took
to answer my questions.
Most of them are mentioned
in the text. Among those who
helped in other capacities
foremost is Sally Dorst, who
did considerable research on
some of the more exotic
examples of penguins in popular culture. The New York
Zoological Society and Sea
World were very helpful, and
thanks go also to my agent,
Kris Dahl, and to Liz Perle,
John Thornton, J. C. Suarès,
and everyone else at
Prentice Hall Press who had
a hand in the book. I don't
want to forget the Society
Expeditions staff members
on the Antarctic cruise I
took, who stood chest-deep
in freezing seas to steady the
rubber landing boats so
tourists like myself could
step out safely into penguin
guano instead of falling into
the water and dying of
hypothermia. And finally, to
my wife and daughters, for
their tolerance of my travels
and working habits, my
heartfelt thanks.

THE TOTAL
PENGUin

Journey to Antarctica to realize the secret life of one of nature's spunkiest, most intriguing, and wackiest creatures! *The Total Penguin* fills the insidious black hole in penguin literature. At once serious and jocular, it combines firsthand experience, natural history, and personal observation in one inspired, witty volume.

Complemented by superb color photographs throughout, writer James Gorman takes us on a delicious romp through the favorite haunts of the penguin. With great humor, the eighteen species of penguin are studiously assessed as to which has given rise to the image of the silly little man in formal attire. Then, without further ado, we are unceremoniously set down in the raucous, raunchy midst of a busy penguin colony. We become privy to how penguins meet, mix, mate, and parent. We witness the dangerous life of the penguin chick. And, we look at the true penguin — an incredibly graceful sea creature who actually flies underwater, using its wings, not feet, to propel itself along.

Gorman also addresses the curious, unfolding history of the centuries-long relationship between penguins and people, wherein the delightful bird has been unfortunately eaten, seriously studied, captured and taken to zoos, and finally, visited in their natural habitat by tourists.

The Total Penguin is, quite simply, a total delight.

James Gorman has been described as "a science writer with the soul of a stand-up comic" (*Boston Globe*), and his playful, informative articles appear in such publications as *The New Yorker*, *Discover*, *The Atlantic*, *The Sciences*, and *Wigwag*. He is the coauthor of *Digging Dinosaurs*, which won the New York Academy of Sciences Children's Science Book Award, and the author of *The Man with No Endorphins: And Other Reflections on Science*. He lives just outside New York City.

Frans Lanting is one of the world's premier wildlife photographers. His photographs appear regularly in leading publications such as *National Geographic*, and he has been honored with numerous international awards.

FRONT COVER: *The rock hopper penguin, with its red eyes, spiked black feathers on the top of its head, and yellow tufted eyebrows, gives a different image than the little man in formal dress. Only a foot high, these birds can be as aggressive as their looks.*

BACK COVER: *A band of gentoo penguins, flippers out, returns from the sea. The undersides of the flippers are flushed pink from increased blood flow, which helps the birds shed heat.*